Confronting Cyberespionage Under International Law

T0373534

We have witnessed a digital revolution that affects the dynamics of existing traditional social, economic, political and legal systems. This revolution has transformed espionage and its features, such as its purpose and targets, methods and means, and actors and incidents, which paves the way for the emergence of the term cyberespionage. This book seeks to address domestic and international legal tools appropriate to adopt in cases of cyberespionage incidents. Cyberespionage operations of state or non-state actors are a kind of cyber attack, which violates certain principles of international law but also constitute wrongful acquisition and misappropriation of the data. Therefore, from the use of force to state responsibility, international law offers a wide array of solutions; likewise, domestic regulations through either specialized laws or general principles stipulate civil and criminal remedies against cyberespionage.

Confronting Cyberespionage Under International Law examines how espionage and its applications have transformed since World War II and how domestic and international legal mechanisms can provide effective legal solutions to this change, hindering the economic development and well-being of individuals, companies and states to the detriment of others. It shows the latest state of knowledge on the topic and will be of interest to researchers, academics, legal practitioners, legal advisors and students in the fields of international law, information technology law and intellectual property law.

Oğuz Kaan Pehlivan, received his B.A. from Bilkent University, Department of Law. He pursued his studies as an exchange student in Katholieke Leuven University, Belgium in 2010–2011. While pursuing his LL.M studies at the unique francophone Galatasaray University in Turkey, he has worked as a lawyer and legal advisor focusing on international law and security in a think-tank environment. In 2014, he was granted a UK Government Chevening Scholarship to pursue his studies at Queen Mary University of London. He is focusing on information technology law, cyber security and applicable international law to cyberspace.

Routledge Research in International Law

For a full list of titles in this series, visit www.routledge.com/Routledge-Research-in-International-Law/book-series/INTNLLAW

Confronting Cyberespionage Under International Law

Oğuz Kaan Pehlivan

Routledge
Taylor & Francis Group

LONDON AND NEW YORK

First published 2019 by Routledge

2 Park Square, Milton Park, Abingdon, Oxfordshire OX14 4RN
52 Vanderbilt Avenue, New York, NY 10017

Routledge is an imprint of the Taylor & Francis Group, an informa business

First issued in paperback 2020

Copyright © 2019 Taylor & Francis

The right of Oğuz Kaan Pehlivan to be identified as author of this work
has been asserted by him in accordance with sections 77 and 78 of the
Copyright, Designs and Patents Act 1988.

All rights reserved. No part of this book may be reprinted or reproduced or
utilised in any form or by any electronic, mechanical, or other means, now
known or hereafter invented, including photocopying and recording, or in
any information storage or retrieval system, without permission in writing
from the publishers.

Notice:
Product or corporate names may be trademarks or registered trademarks,
and are used only for identification and explanation without intent to
infringe.

Library of Congress Cataloging-in-Publication Data
Names: Pehlivan, Oğuz Kaan, author.
Title: Confronting cyberespionage under international
law / Oğuz Kaan Pehlivan.
Description: New York : Routledge, 2018. |
Series: Routledge research in international law |
Includes bibliographical references and index.
Identifiers: LCCN 2018018198 | ISBN 9781138476424 (hbk)
Subjects: LCSH: Espionage. | International law. |
Computer networks–Security measures. | Internet–Security measures. |
Electronic surveillance. | Computer crimes.
Classification: LCC K5252.5 .P45 2018 | DDC 345/.0231–dc23
LC record available at https://lccn.loc.gov/2018018198

ISBN: 978-1-138-47642-4 (hbk)
ISBN: 978-0-367-60682-4 (pbk)

Typeset in Times New Roman
by Out of House Publishing

Dedicated to my family...

Contents

Preface

This study joins a vibrant discussion in the social sciences about one of the challenging issues of cyber security in particular, cyberespionage, as well as appropriate legal responses that might be adopted by victim states. The aim of this study is to investigate and identify economic and industrial cyberespionage and to offer and analyze effective domestic and international legal responses.

We have witnessed a digital revolution, which affects the existing traditional social, economic, political and legal systems around the world globally. This revolution has transformed our interaction with societies and environments. As it is the rule for all new developments, they can offer society an opportunity to ease struggles, but new beginnings are not always clear and certainly not simple. Individuals seek to embrace vast opportunities offered by information technologies as long as they perceive them safe. However, such revolutions have to be addressed by legal mechanisms in order to balance rights-freedoms and the need for security. Espionage activities has also taken its share from the digital revolution. Therefore, this book identifies cyberespionage and the changing features of espionage, such as its purpose and targets, methods and means, and actors and incidents.

This is to show that modern day espionage activities cannot be compared to those people are used to seeing in James Bond or other Hollywood movies. Although espionage seems to have been accepted as a tool adopted by parties of war in times of conflict, actually, espionage and its techniques, mechanisms and tools are dual-use in nature. This nature has been understood, observed and experienced within the past decade because of the proliferation of technology, which paves the way for cyber weapons, attacks, crimes and espionage. We will explain the changing features of espionage in the face of evolving technology. For instance, one of the significant tools frequently adopted by cyberespionage is called APT (Advanced Persistent Threat), which is a sophisticated technique used by hackers to extract large amounts of data from targeted industries over a long period of time. This type of attack is well-tailored for intended sectors or computer networks and has advanced capabilities to extract data and compromise the targeted entity. Such an adversary can spend years to infiltrate documents from the targeted entity without being spotted.

We accepted and built our analysis upon the fact that cyberespionage activities are a kind of cyber attack, which violates intellectual property rights, trade secrets and confidentiality, integrity and sometimes availability of the targeted networks. In addition to that, the focus of this book is on the regulations that seek to address the acts of cyberespionage, which constitute a wrongful acquisition and misappropriation of the data. Many states do not have specific regulations dedicated to tackle cyberespionage so, traditional legal approaches offer to apply regulations covering intellectual property crimes for such activities. Therefore, regulations related to the protection of trade secrets and cybercrimes are domestic legal tools if any private network is targeted by cyberespionage. There are also specific regulations to penalize economic and industrial espionage. Those regulations exist only under the American legal system, so we will also analyze these regulations as well. Concerning domestic regulations, we comparatively analyzed the Turkish and American legal systems in terms of protection of trade secrets and computer crimes.

In terms of international legal responses, we have made a distinction between cyberespionage operations operated by states and non-states actors. With regard to states, we have compared legal responses given and discussed previous sections on wartime and peacetime cyberespionage activities. However, peacetime cyberespionage activities and the appropriate legal responses are the focal points of the study, as they are frequently applied. We argued that cyberespionage activities might be accepted as a form of use of force considering their extremely adverse effects. Moreover, cyber operations need not amount to use of force within the meaning of article 2(4) of the UN Charter to be internationally wrongful, such operations can violate certain obligations and principles of customary international law either. In this sense, cyberespionage activities violate the binding principles of international law, which prohibits interference with the sovereignty and domestic affairs of other states. A state bears international legal responsibility for a cyber operation attributable to it and which constitutes a breach of an international obligation. The basic legal argument to invoke state responsibility with regard to economic cyberespionage is state sovereignty, which also covers the very concept of economic sovereignty.

Whether the operation targets public or private infrastructures, states have sovereignty over both of them. We will argue that cyberespionage operations provide sufficient legal grounds to invoke state responsibility and adopt appropriate measures compatible with internationally wrongful acts, which are considered retorsion and countermeasures covering diplomatic and economic sanctions. Therefore, the first mechanism is declaring responsibility of states for illegitimate acts and responding appropriately.

Furthermore, we have identified that cyberespionage activities can also be conducted before or during bilateral or multilateral treaty negotiations. In this sense, the book argues that the Vienna Convention on the Law of Treaties can provide protection against and play a significant deterrent role for such activities, as they violate the good faith principle and limit the parties' ability to negotiate freely and fairly. Therefore, such violations can trigger invalidity of the treaty by fraud, which is adopted by the Vienna Convention on the Law of Treaties. To illustrate, we have investigated the *Timor-Leste* v. *Australia* case. With regard to the case, violation of both treaty law obligations and established international law norms and principles (inviolability of diplomatic premises, good faith in negotiations, state sovereignty and non-intervention) provide concrete legal basis to assert illegality of cyberespionage. However, establishing the legal and factual link between espionage and fraudulent conduct is complex and problematic due to the lack of any precedent.

With regard to non-state actors, we have asserted that states have certain responsibilities and the victim state can deploy certain offensive measures such as hack back. As economic and industrial cyberespionage activities target intellectual properties, we have discussed legal measures adopted by the Trade-Related Aspects of Intellectual Property Rights (TRIPS) Agreement. Within the limits of World Trade Organization (WTO) agreements, the interpretation of the preamble of the TRIPS Agreement include economic cyberespionage operations within the agreement. As in the commentary of the article 39 of the TRIPS, "a manner contrary to honest commercial practices" has been explained as a "breach of contract, breach of confidence and inducement to breach, and includes the acquisition of undisclosed information by third parties who knew, or were grossly negligent in failing to know, that such practices were involved in the acquisition." Pursuant to the wording of the article, it should be acknowledged that cyberespionage operations are kind of manner contrary to honest commercial practices. However, obligations created by the WTO are only effective and binding within the territories of the parties. Therefore, we have concluded that the WTO dispute resolution mechanism is politically "the most appropriate and effective forum," but legally, parties of the WTO and TRIPS should first agree on international norms and principles explicitly restricting economic cyberespionage operations under WTO agreements.

This book offers several effective legal measures to be adopted by states and corporations on confronting economic and industrial cyberespionage operations and thus makes a small contribution to improve the legal literature on this subject.

Acknowledgements

I would like to express my heart-felt thanks and gratitude to my supervisor Prof. Akif Emre Öktem for his invaluable guidance. I have been amazingly fortunate to have such an advisor who gave me the freedom to explore on my own. I am deeply grateful for his encouragement that helped me sort out the legal details of my work. I would like to thank to Amy Hume for her efforts. I am indebted to my friends for their continuous assistance and feedback.

I should also mention Chevening Scholarship, the UK Government's Global Scholarship Program, funded by the Foreign and Commonwealth Office, which supported my research in London, and other institutions that covered my expenses to attend conferences and courses in Washington DC, London, Paris and Kiev.

I wish to thank the reviewers who responded so positively and the editors at Routledge, especially Gail Welsh and Claire Bell, who worked closely on this project and have given unswerving support.

Most importantly, none of this would have been possible without the support and patience of my wife.

Cases

ICJ, Anglo-Iranian Oil Co. Case (*United Kingdom* v. *Iran*) (Preliminary Objection) (1951)
ICJ, Case Concerning The Continental Shelf (*Libyan Arab Jamahiriya* v. *Malta*) (1985)
E. I Du Pont de Nemours & Company v. *Rolfe Christoper* (1970)
ICJ, Fisheries Jurisdiction Case (*United Kingdom* v. *Iceland*) (Merits) (1974)
ICJ, Gabcikovo-Nagymaros Project (*Hungary* v. *Slovakia*) (1997)
ICJ (*Timor-Leste* v. *Australia*) (Judgment) (2013)
ICJ, Corfu Channel Case (*UK* v. *Albania*) (1949)
ICJ, Military and Paramilitary Activities in and Against Nicaragua (*Nicaragua* v. *US*) (1984)
Mars UK Ltd v. *Teknowledge Ltd* (1999)
ICJ, The Barcelona Traction (*Belgium* v. *Spain*) (1970)
ICJ, The Case of the S.S. Lotus (*France* v. *Turkey*) (1927)
ICJ, North Sea Continental Shelf Case (*Germany* v. *Denmark*; *Germany* v. *Netherland*) (1969)
ICJ, Nuclear Tests Case (*Australia* v. *France*) (Merits) (1974)
ICJ, Rainbow Warrior (*New Zealand* v. *France*) (1990)
PCA, *Timor-Leste* v. *Australia* (2013)
PCIJ, Phosphates in Morocco (Judgment) (1938)
Sheridan v. *Mallinckrodt, Inc.*, 568 F. Supp. 1347
United States v. *Michael J. Oberhard* (1989)
United States v. *Aleynikov* (2012)
United States v. *Caesar Bottone, Seymour Salb, and Nathan Sharff* (1966)
United States v. *Wang Dong, Sun Kai Liang, Wen Xinyu, Huang Zhenyu, Gu Chunhi* (2014)
Yargıtay, 11. C.D., 26.03.2009, E.2008/18190 K. 2009/3058
Yargıtay, 11. HD., E.2004/7827; K.2007/5755

Abbreviations

AFCEA	Armed Forces Communication and Electronics Association
AFDIA	Annuaire Français de Droit International Année
ANSSI	L'agence Nationale de la Sécurité des Systèmes d'Information
APT	advanced persistent threat
ASD	Australian Signals Directorate
ASIO	Australian Security Intelligence Organization
ASIS	Australian Secret Intelligence Service
ASIL	American Society of International Law
ASEAN	Association of Southeast Asian Nations
COMINT	Communications Intelligence
CNO	computer network operations
CCDCOE	NATO Cooperative Cyber Defense Committee of Excellence
CNA	computer network attack
CND	computer network defense
CNE	computer network exploitation
CSEC	Communications Security Establishment Canada
CMAT	Certain Maritime Arrangements in the Timor Sea
DJILP	*Denver Journal of International Law and Policy*
EJIL	*European Journal of International Law*
EU	European Union
FISA	Foreign Intelligence Surveillance Act
GCHQ	UK Government Communications Headquarters
GCSB	Government Communications Security Bureau
GJICLR	*Georgia Journal of International and Comparative Law Review*
HILJ	*Harvard International Law Journal*
HUMINT	human intelligence

HPCR	Harvard Program on Humanitarian Policy and Conflict Research
ICJ	International Court of Justice
IP address	Internet Protocol address
ILC	International Law Commissions
ICLQ	*International and Comparative Law Quarterly*
JIPLP	*Journal of Intellectual Property Law and Practice*
MJIL	*Michigan Journal of International Law*
NIST	National Institute of Standards and Technology
NSA	US National Security Agency
NGO	non-governmental organization
para.	paragraph
PCA	Permanent Court of Arbitration
PCIJ	Permanent Court of International Justice
PLC	Programmable Logic Controllers
PLA	Chinese People's Liberation Army
RUSI	Royal United Services Institute
SIGINT	Signals Intelligence
SCADA	Supervisory Control and Data Acquisition
SANS	Escal Institute of Advanced Technologies
SOE	state-owned enterprise
TPC	Turkish Penal Code with n. 5271
TCC	Turkish Commercial Code with n. 6102
TRIPS	Trade-Related Aspects of Intellectual Property Rights
USA/US	United States of America
USCC	US–CHINA Economic and Security Review Commission
UN	United Nations
UNDP	United Nations Development Program
UKUSA	United Kingdom – United States of America Agreement
UNTS	United Nation Treaty Series
UTSA	Uniform Trade Secrets Act
YILC	*Yearbook of the International Law Commission*
VCLT	Vienna Convention on the Law of Treaties
VJIL	*Virginia Journal of International Law*
WTO	World Trade Organization

Introduction

The computer will condition every facet of human life in the future and so far as law is used to regulate that life it will affect the development of the law.[1]

Rapid developments in Internet and information technologies since the 1990s have not only changed our daily lives but also have transformed the way we perceive the world. Initial signs of this change can be traced back to 1980s when the cost of storing data was reduced and personal computers began to be used widely.[2] The first computers were used mostly to process data and for calculation purposes. This traditional and limited relation between user and device demonstrated one-way interaction which was destined to evolve into a larger, comprehensive cyber environment, together with further developments in the field. Therefore, with the launch of blogs and portals people started to interact with each other and every individual appeared to be an active player creating a multifaceted interactive platform. This shift to personal computers and Internet usage helped Internet and information technologies create a massive economy. According to the Boston Consulting Group, "By 2016, there will be 3 billion Internet users globally and the Internet economy will reach $4.2 trillion in the G-20 economies."[3] In other words, the Internet economy will rank among the world's top five

---

1 Colin Tapper, *Computers and the Law*, London: Weidenfeld and Nicolson (1973), xv.
2 In 1956 it cost 50,000 USD to buy the world's first hard drive which stores 5MB of data. By 1980 a 26 MD HDD cost 5,000 USD. In 1987 a 40MB HDD was 1,799 USD. By the 1995 2.9 MB HDD became 2,899 USD which cost 85 cents per MB. Nowadays the price per MD of HDD has dropped to 0.008 cents. For more information see: *Historical Notes about the Cost of Hard Drive Storage Space* http://ns1758.ca/winch/winchest. html.
3 The Boston Consulting Group Inc., *The Internet Economy in the G-20*, Boston: BCG (2012), 1.

economies. As Murray stated, we have experienced a massive digitization process in every corner and have witnessed the spread of computers in various areas from finance to health, water management to electricity distribution lines/grids, personal messaging to diplomatic messaging, and so on.[4] Cate describe this phenomenon: "we are witnessing an explosion in digital data."[5] However, the negative side is that these developments continue to occupy our individual and professional lives. Even though those changes have altered communication and information technologies and erased many challenges from our lives to a great extent, they also have paved the way for proliferation of new kinds of threats and crimes.

Throughout the history, new technological developments empowered many people to the detriment of existing and traditional power structures.[6] Likewise, given the nature of the cyberspace, cross-border cyber-attacks and cybercrimes become new challenges which threaten our security. Many of the states mentioned cybercrimes and cyber-attacks in their national cyber strategy policy papers. Especially in the UK, cybercrime is one of the founding pillars of the national cyber strategy and is among its highest priorities.[7] This rising phenomenon creates several problems in terms of economy, politics, law and technics and cooperation. Thanks to the easy and inexpensive access opportunities to computers and Internet connections, standalone criminals or state-backed entities can initiate cross-border cyber-attacks successfully. They target national critical infrastructures such as finance and banking networks or flight control systems, which results in devastating harm to states and individuals.

In addition to cybercrimes and cyber-attacks, today almost every nation suffers from cyberespionage, technically named computer network exploitation.[8] The underlying reason for that is the change in

---

4 Andrew Murray, *Information Technology Law*, Oxford: Oxford University Press (2013), 5.
5 Fred H. Cate, *Privacy in the Information Age*, Washington, DC: Brookings Institute Press (1997), 16.
6 Eric Schmidt and Jared Cohen, *The New Digital Age: Reshaping the Future of People, Nations and Business*, New York: Vintage Books (2013), 6–7; Moises Naim, *End of Power: From Boardrooms to Battlefields and Churches to States, Why Being in Charge isn't What it Used to Be*, New York: Basic Books (2013), 13–14; Henry Kissinger, *World Order*, London: Penguin Books (2014), 341–47.
7 UK government, "A Strong Britain in an Age of Uncertainty: The National Security Strategy" (2010), 27.
8 Katherine L. Herbig and Martin F. Wiskoff, *Espionage Against the United States by American Citizens 1947–2001*, Monterey: Defense Personnel Security Research Center

known patterns of espionage within a decade. Along with its methods and means, its targets and purpose have fundamentally changed. The ultimate purpose and target of the operations have become to acquire company data, which includes personal data, confidential data and intellectual property data consisting of business secrets, R&D documents, cutting-edge technological plans and so on. Second, while human-based intelligence and espionage operations (HUMINT)[9] have decreased in importance, signal-based intelligence and espionage operations (SIGINT and COMINT)[10] have enormously proliferated given the changes in technological capabilities. Espionage is a grey and controversial area of international law, thus every nation regulates espionage under their criminal codes. However the matter of responding to or punishing the espionage, especially cyberespionage activities mostly based on APT (Advanced Persistent Threat) attacks, constitutes a remarkable aspect of the issue and there are more and more concrete, visible actions taken to prevent it. Due to the radical increase of cyberattacks and espionage operations, states are looking for effective legal mechanisms to tackle them. Victim states can condemn the targeting state and initiate naming and shaming campaigns against espionage operations, but they are also looking for other legal mechanisms such as invoking state responsibility, asserting violation of treaty obligations and seeking reparation and compensation.

This research analytically and legally examines and attempts to find an answer to the question of how states can confront economic and industrial cyberespionage activities under existing international law mechanisms.

(2002), 80: "Globalization is rapidly creating new international conditions based on global economics that will affect the allegiance of citizens. This development assures that economic espionage will become more important as dual-use Technologies blur the distinction between national defense and industrial applications."
9 EU Parliament, Report on the Existence of A Global System for the Interception of Private and Commercial Communications (ECHELON interception system) (2001/2098(INI)): "Protection of secret information is always organized in the same way: 1) only a small number of people, who have been vetted, have access to secret information 2) there are established rules for dealing with such information 3) normally the information does not leave the protected area, and if it does so, it leaves only in a secure manner or encrypted form. The prime method of carrying out organized espionage is therefore by gaining access to the desired information directly through people ('human intelligence'). These may be: 4) plants (agents) acting on behalf of the service/business engaging in espionage 5) people recruited from the target area."
10 Ibid., "The form of espionage by technical means with which electromagnetic signals of any kind are intercepted and analyzed ('signals intelligence', SIGINT)."

1 Cyberspace, espionage and cyberespionage

> What are the social and private interest that the law should recognize and protect? Here technological change set new problems and gave new urgency to old ones. The law had to alter many definitions of what was private and what was the public interest. The law has almost always been acted upon by, or has responded to, technological change, rather than controlled it.[1]

"What was the most significant advancement that affected social, political, economic and legal systems fundamentally in the early 21st century?" This will be the question asked by 22nd-century historians. They will try to answer that question by looking at various developments that affect society, politics, economics, and legal systems, but also their meaning, function, and nature. They will possibly acknowledge the revolution in information technologies, which is defined as the use of systems for storing, retrieving, and sending information. This revolution is two-fold: first, the cost of storing information sharply decreases, and second, connection speed, and cost decrease dramatically.

Expanded access to information and the widespread usage of social media tools and the Internet has fundamentally altered the interaction between people and their environment. This accelerated and freed the dissemination of information, accurate or not, about any issue or fact. On the other hand, the protection of valuable information became more challenging due to the lack of security inherent to information technologies, as they are not intended to provide security, but to create alternative communication challenges, which provide impregnable access.[2]

---

1 James Williard Hurst, *The Growth of American Law: The Law Makers*, Boston: Little Brown and Company (1950), 10.
2 David Sutcliffe, "What are the current grand challenges of internet research," Oxford Internet Institute Blog (2016): "The technologies that affect us are changing far faster

In this context, defining cyberspace and its components is significant in regards to providing regulation while protecting fundamental rights and freedoms, and to tackle criminals and threats effectively. This freedom-security balance is the key to regulate cyberspace. Governments would like to regulate cyberspace heavily to increase their control by asserting security concerns; individuals or oppositions will challenge and protest such regulations as they are suggested to the detriment of freedom of expression or right to receive information. When it comes to regulating espionage, there is no hesitation and objection raised from either side. However, espionage activities have undergone a fundamental transformation along with the above-mentioned revolution.[3] Therefore, this chapter will analyze and evaluate the transformation in purposes, means, targets, and actors of espionage. This quest will constitute a basis to analyze cyberespionage, to define its legal characteristics and how to respond legally. This chapter will first offer a definition of cyberspace and further elaborate on its regulation. Second, it will comparatively analyze positive and negative views on regulating peacetime espionage activities in order to provide a legal basis regarding international legal responses to peacetime cyberespionage activities.

Regulating cyberspace and espionage

Challenges inherent to regulating cyberspace

Defining cyberspace

"Relating to or characteristic of the culture of computers, information technology, and virtual reality," is the definition of "cyber" according to Oxford Dictionary.[4] Cyberspace has become a widely used notion; however, the terminology to describe it is still developing. William Gibson,

than at any previous time in the history; They are also being adopted at breakneck pace, i.e. faster than we can catch up, and this has unseen implications. The technology sector is used to asking, 'can we build it and make money?' and dealing with the societal implications later."

3 Katherine L. Herbig and Martin F. Wiskoff, *Espionage Against the United States by American Citizens 1947–2001*, Monterey, CA: Defense Personnel Security Research Center (2002), 79: "The current revolution in information and communications technologies is changing the scope and practices of espionage: spy's method of collection, synthesis and transmission of information are shifting to take advantage of opportunities in these new technologies."

4 *Oxford English Dictionary*, Oxford: Oxford University Press, 7 (2013), 173.

a science fiction writer, was the first to use the term "cyberspace" within his science fiction novel written in 1984.[5] A review of government and scholarly literature reveals the difficulty of providing a conclusive and comprehensive definition of cyberspace that covers all of its functionality. In academia, Norbert Wiener first used the term cybernetics in 1948,[6] and in 1999, Lance Strate gave an early definition of cyberspace as a collective concept of "the diverse experiences of space associated with computing and related technologies."[7] Ottis and Lorents defined cyberspace as a "time-dependent set of interconnected information systems and the human users that interact where users, nodes, and connections can appear and disappear and the information is transformed over time."[8] A comprehensive definition was offered by Kuehl, according to which cyberspace is "a global domain within the information environment whose distinctive and unique character is framed by the use of electronics and the electromagnetic spectrum to create, store, modify, exchange, and exploit information via interdependent and interconnected networks using information communication technologies."[9]

Cyberspace is defined by the United States Department of Defense (US DoD) as a global domain within the information environment consisting of the interdependent networks of information technology infrastructures and resident data, including the Internet, telecommunications networks, computer systems, and embedded processors and controllers.[10] It is also described in terms of three layers: 1) a physical network, 2) a logical network, and 3) a cyber-persona layer:

- The physical network is composed of the geographic and physical network components.
- The logical network consists of related elements abstracted from the physical network.

5 William Gibson, *Neuromancer*, New York: Ace Publishing (1984), 4. ("A year here and he still dreamed of cyberspace, hope fading nightly.")

6 Norbert Wiener, *Cybernetics, Second Edition: or the Control and Communication in the Animal and the Machine*, Massachusetts: MIT Press (1948).

7 Lance Strate, "The varieties of cyberspace: problems in definition and delimitation," *Western Journal of Communication*, 63 (1999), 383.

8 R. Ottis and P. Lorents, "Cyberspace: definition and implications," in *Proceedings of the 5th International Conference on Information Warfare and Security*, Dayton: Reading, UK: Academic Publishing Limited (2010), 267–70.

9 Daniel T. Kuehl, "From cyber space to cyberpower: defining the problem," in Franklin D. Kramer, Stuart H. Starr and Larry K. Wentz, *Cyberpower and National Security*, Washington, DC: National Defense University Press (2009), 28.

10 Department of Defense Joint Publications 3–12, *Cyberspace Operations* (2013) www.jcs.mil/Portals/36/Documents/Doctrine/pubs/jp3_12R.pdf.

• The cyber-persona layer uses the rules of the logical network layer to develop a digital representation of an individual or entity identity.

As for the National Institute of Standards and Technology (NIST), cyberspace is "a global domain within the information environment consisting of the interdependent network of information systems' infrastructures including the Internet, telecommunications networks, computer systems, and embedded processors and controllers."[11] According to Turkey's National Cyber Security Strategy and 2013–2014 Action Plan, cyberspace is "the environment which consists of information systems that span across the world including the networks that interconnect these systems."[12] According to the UK Cyber Security Strategy, cyberspace is "an interactive domain made up of digital networks that are used to store, modify and communicate information. It includes the Internet, but also the other information systems that support our businesses, infrastructure and services."[13] According to the L'agence Nationale de la Sécurité des Systèmes d'Information (ANSSI) cyberspace is "espace de communication constitué par l'interconnexion mondiale d'équipements de traitement automatisé de données numériques."[14] In other words, cyberspace is the communication space created by the worldwide interconnection of automated digital data processing equipment. Therefore, key components of cyberspace can be defined and categorized as technology, complexity, and human components along with its global nature.

In this regard, we simply prefer the definition of cyberspace as the "realm of computer networks (and the users behind them) in which information is stored, shared and communicated online."[15] Although all of the above definitions except that given by US DoD explain cyberspace as a virtual world, it is more than virtual and has a physical dimension. All human activity, this includes actions in cyberspace, happens in the physical world. People log into computers and online services with regard to their geographical location; computers are addressed through domain names (such as www.abc.com) which give no indication of physical location, but the knowledge containing that domain name is

---

11 Richard Kissel (ed.), *NIST Glossary of Key Information Security Terms*, Gaithersburg: National Institute of Standards and Technology (2013), 58.
12 Turkey's National Cyber Security and 2013–2014 Action Plan (2012).
13 The UK Cyber Security Strategy: protecting and promoting the UK in a digital world (2011).
14 ANSSI Glossaries, see www.ssi.gouv.fr/administration/glossaire/c/.
15 P. W. Singer and Allan Friedman, *Cybersecurity and Cyberwar: What Everyone Needs to Know*, Oxford: Oxford University Press (2014), 13.

physically located in a server elsewhere.[16] Paying attention to the physical dimension element is significant, because the espionage operations intent is to try to steal the information stored within physical entities.

Regulating cyberspace

Ideas on regulating cyberspace have been changing since the 1990s, due to increased risks and threats. Early scholars proposed the idea of cyber exceptionalism or cyber libertarianism, which defined cyberspace as transnational, far from regulations and a place where existing "legal concepts of property, expression, identity, movement, and context do not apply to."[17] Other scholars opposed this idea; for example, Reed points out that there is fallacy behind cyber exceptionalism because "all the actors involved in an Internet transaction have a real-world existence and are located in one or more legal jurisdictions. It's inconceivable that a real-world jurisdiction would deny that its laws potentially applied to the transaction."[18] If traditional law enforcement bodies have faced the challenge of cross-border trade or harm, the ordinary rules of private international law, jurisdiction and choice of law have proven effective in identifying the correct forum and legal rules to apply.[19]

Even earlier, Goldsmith pointed out that cyber skeptics made three basic mistakes, which are an overstatement of cyberspace transactions, disregarding "the distinction between default laws and mandatory laws," and underestimation of the capability of existing legal tools and techniques.[20] Besides Brown's argument that "cyberspace is nowhere,"[21] according to Dinniss (and our view), "there does not exist some

---

16 Dorothy E. Denning and Peter F. MacDoran, "Grounding cyberspace in the physical world," in Alan D. Campen, Douglas H. Dearth and R. Thomas Goodden (eds.), *Cyberwar: Security, Strategy and Conflict in the Information Age*, Fairfax: AFCEA International Press (1996), 119.

17 John Perry Barlow, "A declaration of the independence of cyberspace," California: Electronic Frontier Foundation (1996) https://projects.eff.org/~barlow/Declaration-Final.html (accessed 18 July 2015); David Johnson and David Post, "Law and borders – the rise of law in cyberspace," *Stanford Law Review*, 48 (1996), 1367; Andrew Murray, *Information Technology Law*, Oxford: Oxford University Press (2013), 56.

18 Chris Reed, *Internet Law: Text and Materials*, Cambridge: Cambridge University Press (2004), 175.

19 Reed, *Internet Law*, 176; Murray, *Information Technology Law*, 57.

20 Jack L. Goldsmith, "Against cyberanarchy," *University of Chicago Law Review*, 65(4) (1998), 1200.

21 Davis Brown, "A proposal for an international convention to regulate the use of information systems in armed conflict," *HILJ*, 47 (2006), 179.

'matrix-like' realm of cyberspace which bears no connection to the 'real world.' Actors still act in physical space; hardware and networks (even wireless and virtual ones) still require physical constructs."[22] In the case of international law and cyberspace challenges, US State Department Legal Advisor Harold Koh also opposed the idea of cyber exceptionalism in 2012. In his speech, Koh stated that established norms and principles of international law are applicable to cyberspace and cyberspace is not a law-free zone, but also set the fundamental question with regard to armed conflict, sovereignty, self-defense, cyber weapons, etc.[23] Even before Koh's speech, some scholars underlined that existing international law norms and principles, especially designed for *jus ad bellum* and *jus in bello*, can provide a normative framework to cope with legal problems posed by cyberspace.[24] Nevertheless, even existing legal tools and techniques should be revised, improved and interpreted to embrace the new challenges emerging due to technological advancement.[25] For instance, the concept of war has undergone a transformation since the 1900s. Its nature, definition, techniques, and elements have begun to change due to developments in technology. The often-quoted definition of war was underlined by L. Oppenheim, who stated several elements: "war is contention between two or more states through their armed force, for the purpose of overpowering each other and imposing such conditions of peace as the victor pleases."[26]

Within the last two decades, this definition has deteriorated and become limited only to one type of conflict[27] far from embracing the

22 Heather Harrison Dinniss, *Cyber Warfare and the Laws of War*, Cambridge: Cambridge University Press (2012), 28.
23 Harold H. Koh, "International law in cyberspace," The USCYBERCOM Inter-Agency Legal Conference (2012) www.state.gov/s/l/releases/remarks/197924.htm (accessed 18 July 2015).
24 Michael N. Schmitt, "Computer network attack and the use of force in international law: thoughts on a normative framework," *Columbia Journal of Transnational Law*, 37 (1999), 885; Dinniss, *Cyber Warfare and the Laws of War*, 9; see William M. Stahl, "The uncharted waters of cyberspace: applying the principles of international maritime law to the problem of cybersecurity," *GJICLR*, 40 (2011), 247–73.
25 As the neorealism theory of international relations accept that power is the most important factor in international relations and therefore challenge the existing legal norms and offer new interpretations, this understanding spread through the regulation of cyberspace as well.
26 Lassa Oppenheim, *International Law, a Treatise II*, New York: Longmans, Green and Co. (first published 1912), 61.
27 Yoram Dinstein, *War, Aggression and Self Defence*, Cambridge: Cambridge University Press, 5th ed. (2011), 12: "Oppenheim's definition postulates what is termed nowadays a 'total' war. Many a war is unquestionably 'total' in that it is conducted with total victory

others.[28] For example, intra-state conflicts have increased in number, concepts like violent non-state actors or international foreign fighters have been proposed, and just as information warfare or cyber warfare, cyberespionage has come to light. Still, this does not mean that Oppenheim's definition, likewise principles of armed conflict (*jus in bello*) or principles of *jus ad bellum*, is not adequate to cover new kinds of conflict, but their elements should be interpreted in the light of new advancements.[29]

In this context, on the one hand, existing international law norms and principles should be interpreted concerning cross-border cyberespionage operations and activities, and new rules should be prepared to combat this new threat on the other.

Regulating espionage

Although it is called the second oldest profession in history[30] and has been practiced since the dawn of human history,[31] espionage is an

in mind. Total victory consists of the capitulation of the enemy, following the overall defeat of its armed forces and/or the conquest of its territory, and if this is accomplished the victor is capable of dictating peace terms to the vanquished. Not every war is aimed at total victory. Oppenheim completely overlooked the feasibility of limited wars. Such wars are, in fact, of considerable frequency and import. In a limited war, the goal may be confined to the defeat of only some segments of the opposing military apparatus; the conquest of certain portions of the opponent's territory (and no others); or the coercion of the enemy Government to alter a given policy without striving for total victory."

28 Further see: Rosa Brooks, *How Everything Became War and the Military Became Everything*, New York: Simon & Schuster (2016), 4: "I sensed something disturbing: all our fine new technologies and fine new legal theories were blurring the boundaries of war, causing it to spread and ooze into everyday life. the U.S. government has also made it clear that it views cyber threats primarily through the lens of war." White House, An International Strategy for Cyberspace (2011), www.whitehouse.gov/sites/default/files/rss_viewer/international_strategy_for_cyberspace.pdf.: declaring that the United States would "respond to hostile acts in cyberspace as we would any other threat to our country." Harold H. Koh, "International law in cyberspace": "cyber activities may in certain circumstances constitute uses of force, triggering the law of armed conflict and giving rise to a right to respond with traditional physical force."
29 See, Marco Roscini, *Cyber Operations and the Use of Force in International Law*, Oxford: Oxford University Press (2014); Marco Roscini, "World wide warfare – jus ad Bellum and the use of cyber force," *Max Planck Yearbook of United Nations Law*, 14 (2010), 96; Yoram Dinstein, "The principle of distinction and cyber war in international armed conflicts," *Journal of Conflict and Security Law*, 17(2) (2012), 261–77; Yoram Dinstein, "Cyber war and international law: concluding remarks at the 2012 Naval War College International Law Conference," *International Law Studies*, 89 (2013), 276.
30 Phillip Knightley, *The Second Oldest Profession: Spies and Spying in the Twentieth Century*, New York: W. W. Norton & Co. (1986).
31 Katharina Ziolkowski, "Peacetime cyber espionage – new tendencies in public international law," in Katharina Ziolkowski (ed.), *Peacetime Regime for State Activities*

evolving and dynamic concept, capable of adjusting itself to a changing environment. Apart from its application, methods, and means, the legality of espionage activities is one of the disputed topics of law. Moral and legal rules in peacetime are radically different from rules in wartime. Therefore, international legal scholars have different opinions about deciding whether intelligence activities are permitted or restricted by international law as it is applicable in peacetime or wartime.[32] Some scholars argued that these activities have been prohibited, others argued that it has been permitted, while still others described espionage activities as a gray area, being neither regulated nor permitted.

Along with the academics, in cases of wartime espionage activities, several international law documents set out restrictions. Accordingly, the Geneva Convention of 1949[33] and the 1977 Additional Protocol I to the Geneva Conventions[34] embedded several articles imposing restrictions upon wartime espionage and penalties for captured spies.[35] Alternatively, in cases of peacetime espionage – as it is not defined by any international law instruments – international law treated it as being outside the scope of the law and did not not impose any restrictions on on it or on intelligence collection activities.[36] However, it should be the other way around, because,

in Cyberspace: International Law, International Relations and Diplomacy CCDCOE (2013), 425.

32 See international law restrict espionage activities in peacetime: Quincy Wright, "Espionage and the doctrine of non-intervention in internal affairs," edited by R. J. Stanger, *Essays on Espionage and International Law*, Ohio: Ohio State University Press (2008). See international law permit espionage activities in peacetime: W. Hays Parks, "The international law of intelligence collection," in John Norton Moore and Robert F. Turner (eds.), *National Security Law*, Durham: Carolina Academic Press (1999), 433–34; Geoffrey B. Demarest, "Espionage in international law," *DJILP*, 24 (1996), 321; A. John Radsan, "The unresolved equation of espionage and international law," *MJIL*, 28 (2007), 595; Jens David Ohlin, Kevin Govern and Claire Finkelstein, *Cyber War: Law and Ethics for Virtual Conflicts*, Oxford: Oxford University Press (2015).

33 Geneva Convention Relative to the Protection of Civilian Persons in Time of War (adopted on 12 August 1949, entered into force 21 October 1950), 75 U.N.T.S 287 art. 5.

34 Protocol Additional to the Geneva Conventions of 12 August 1949, and relating to the Protection of Victims of International Armed Conflict (Protocol I) (adopted 8 June 1977), 1125 U.N.T.S. 3 arts 45, 46.

35 Dieter Fleck, "Individual and state responsibility for intelligence gathering," *MJIL*, 28 (2007), 687.

36 John Kish and David Turns (eds), *International Law and Espionage*, New York: Kluwer Law International (1995); John Yoo, "Counterintuitive: intelligence operations and international law," *MJIL*, 28 (2006), 626; Geoffrey B. Demarest, "Espionage in international law," *DJILP*, 24 (1996), 321; Luke Pelican, "Peacetime cyberespionage: a

technically, the law of war is referred to using the Latin term *lex specialis* – specific law. It is applicable in – and only in – special circumstances, but in those special circumstances, it supersedes the ordinary law, or *lex generalis*, the "general law" that prevails in peacetime. We have one set of laws for 'normal' situations, and another, more flexible set of laws for "extraordinary" situations, such as armed conflicts.[37]

In this sense, we will discuss the problems and challenges regarding regulation of espionage activities under international law.

Legality of wartime espionage activities

Wartime espionage activities are allowed and regulated by several international legal documents. It is clearly stated under article 119 of HPCR Manual on International Law Applicable to Air and Missile Warfare that "Acts of espionage are not prohibited under the law of international armed conflict."[38] Similarly, one of the early documents from the Hague Convention on respecting the Laws and Customs of War on Land states: "ruses of war and the employment of measures necessary for obtaining information about the enemy and the country are considered permissible."[39] This Convention also set out rules for spies and espionage activities. According to article 39 of the Protocol Additional (I) to the Geneva Conventions (12 August 1949), and Relating to the Protection of Victims of International Armed Conflicts,[40] it is acknowledged that there are rules applicable to espionage. This article paves the way for

dangerous, but necessary game," *CommLaw Conspectus*, 20 (2012), 363; Christopher S. Yoo, "Cyber espionage or cyber war?: International law, domestic law and self-protective measures," *Faculty Scholarship Paper*, 1540 (2015) http://scholarship.law.upenn.edu/faculty_scholarship/1540 (accessed 27 July 2015).

37 Kristen Boon and Douglas Lovelace, *Terrorism: Commentary on Security Documents Volume 133. The Drone Wars of the 21st century: Costs and Benefits*, Oxford: Oxford University Press (2014), 140.

38 HPCR, *Manual on International Law Applicable to Air and Missile Warfare*, Harvard University (2009), 42 https://reliefweb.int/sites/reliefweb.int/files/resources/8B2E79FC145BFB3D492576E00021ED34-HPCR-may2009.pdf (accessed 4 May 2018).

39 Hague Convention on respecting the Laws and Customs of War on Land (entered into force 26 January 1910), art. 24.

40 Protocol Additional to the Geneva Conventions of 12 August 1949, and Relating to the Protection of Victims of International Armed Conflicts (Protocol I). "1. It is prohibited to make use in an armed conflict of the flags or military emblems, insignia or uniforms of neutral or other States not parties to the conflict. 2. It is prohibited to

applicability of generally recognized rules of international law to espionage through legal analogy. Based on this reasoning, we will try to examine the application of existing legal frameworks to new types of espionage activities.

Furthermore, regarding article 46 of the same protocol, named "Spies," specific provisions were set out for regulating espionage activities.[41] First, this article states that if someone was captured while engaging in espionage, they shall not have the right to enjoy the status of prisoners of war and may be treated as a spy. Second, attempts to gather information shall not be considered as engaging in espionage if that person is in the uniform of his armed forces. Third, the article states that to gather, or attempts to gather, information of military value within that territory shall not be considered as engaging in espionage unless that person does so through an act of false pretenses or deliberately in a clandestine manner.

Legal statutes of spies and espionage activities during times of war crystallized in these international legal documents. However, even before the enactment of these documents, several scholars argued about the legal status of spies and espionage activities. Pioneering international law scholar Hugo Grotius has mentioned spies and activities

make use of the flags or military emblems, insignia or uniforms of adverse Parties while engaging in attacks or in order to shield, favor, protect or impede military operations. 3. Nothing in this *Article* or in Article 37, paragraph one (d), shall affect the existing generally recognized rules of international law applicable to espionage or to the use of flags."

41 Notwithstanding any other provision of the Conventions or of this Protocol, any member of the armed forces of a Party to the conflict who falls into the power of an adverse Party while engaging in espionage shall not have the right to the status of prisoners of war and may be treated as a spy.

A member of the armed forces of a Party to the conflict who, on behalf of that Party and in territory controlled by an adverse Party, gathers or attempts to gather information shall not be considered as engaging in espionage if, while so acting, he is in the uniform of his armed forces.

A member of the armed forces of a Party to the conflict who is a resident of territory occupied by an adverse Party and who, on behalf of the Party on which he depends, gathers or attempts to gather information of military value within that territory shall not be considered as engaging in espionage unless he does so through an act of false pretenses or deliberately in a clandestine manner. Moreover, such a resident shall not lose his right to the status of prisoners of war and may not be treated as a spy unless he is captured while engaging in espionage.

A member of the armed forces of a Party to the conflict who is not a resident of territory occupied by an adverse Party and who has engaged in espionage in that territory shall not lose his right to the status of prisoners of war and may not be treated as a spy unless he is captured before he has rejoined the armed forces to which he belongs.

of espionage in his cornerstone book, *On the Law of War and Peace*. According to Grotius:

> For so are Spies used, yet it is held lawful, by the general Consent of Nations, to send such, as Moses did, and such was Joshua himself and that justly sometimes, by such as have manifestly a lawful Cause to make War, by others with Impunity, which the Law of Arms grants.[42]

In the same book translated and published by another author, Grotius explained the same topic:

> …there is no doubt, but the law of nations allows anyone to send spies, as Moses did to the land of promise, of whom Joshua was one. Persons of that description may sometimes be lawfully employed by those, who are engaged in an evidently just war. Others too, who have not such evident proofs of the justice of their cause, may plead the rights of war as a vindication for employing such persons.[43]

First of all, it is crucial to keep in mind while commenting on those paragraphs that Grotius has described this rule (allowance or consent of nations) at a time when human-to-human intelligence (human-based intelligence) is commonly employed and spying is a profession performed only by an individual without requiring any additional technical tools. However, today, almost all modern intelligence techniques require a minimum human-to-human interaction but are applied through technological devices.

Furthermore, according to Grotius, employing someone as a spy is lawful in the case of "evidently *just war*" situations, if there is not any evidence for justification of espionage, then the rights of war can be applied. There is only one option for employing a spy for Grotius, which is the state of being in war or intention of such. While Grotius stated, "For so are Spies used, yet it is held lawful, by the general Consent of Nations," he was clearly arguing the lawfulness of such general consent in the case of being in a state of war. Additionally, he made this explanation and discussed the topic under Chapter 4, titled: "On the Right of Killing an Enemy in Lawful War and Committing Other

---

42 Hugo Grotius, *The Rights of War and Peace*, Book 3, edited by Knud Haakonssen, Indianapolis: Liberty Fund (2005), 1295.
43 Hugo Grotius, *On the Law of War and Peace*, translated and edited by A. C. Campbell, Kitchener: Batoche Books (2001), 289.

Acts of Hostility." In other words, Grotius argued espionage activities conducted during a time of war and categorized such activities as acts of lawful hostility. Therefore, Grotius considered lawful espionage activities during times of war but remained quiet for peacetime espionage activities and under which circumstances employing spies and conducting espionage activities can be perceived as lawful and just. To this end, espionage activities and spying in times of war are regulated at an international level. There is little doubt whether these activities are subject to any kind of sanctions. However, the legality and consequences of peacetime espionage activities are still controversial and such activities are widely applied after the establishment of the UN system, prohibition of the use of force and threats.[44]

Legality of peacetime espionage activities

According to Falk, "traditional international law is remarkably oblivious to the peacetime practice of espionage. As for the Radsan, espionage is operating in a sort of legal twilight."[45] "Leading treatises overlook espionage altogether or contain a perfunctory paragraph that defines a spy and describes his hapless fate in the event of capture. Yet espionage has always played a prominent role in international relations."[46] This statement indicates two points; first, there is not any rule or principle proposed by traditional international law. To illustrate, the doctrine – called the *Lotus Principle* – laid down by the Permanent Court of International Justice in the Lotus case underlines that restrictions upon states cannot be presumed. In the absence of prohibitive rules, each state is free to adopt any approach or act accordingly.[47] Therefore, it is proposed that espionage is an area, where there is no prohibitive applicable law. *Non liquet* is the legal terminology used to describe this situation. However, we should emphasize that although the *Lotus Principle* represents a general attitude towards peacetime espionage operations, this principle became questionable with regard to peacetime cyberespionage operations. Deeks explained this activity

---

44 With the establishment of prohibition of use of force, legal scholars abandon to separate international law as peacetime and wartime. Peacetime accepted to become the settled and dominate reality although there have been many conflicts. Scholars changed their terminology. However their shift in terminology did not suffice to end the use of force, conflicts and armed attacks.

45 Radsan, "The unresolved equation of espionage," 595.

46 Richard A. Falk, "Forward," in Roland J. Stranger (ed.), *Essays on Espionage and International Law*, Ohio: Ohio State University Press (1962), 107.

47 PCIJ, The Case of the S.S. Lotus (*France* v. *Turkey*) Series A. No. 10 (1927).

as international law agnosticism and stressed that we are experiencing a shift from agnosticism because of Snowden's revelations.[48] In this regard, state practices creating customary international law restricting such activities are emerging, on the one hand, and on the other hand soft law is emerging at international and regional levels (as the case in EU).

CUSTOMARY INTERNATIONAL LAW AND ESPIONAGE

In the early years of international law, customary law was the primary tool of creating norms, which gave treaties a secondary importance.[49] Despite the fact that it had to leave its prestigious prevailing status to the law of treaties, considering international law has never been off the table.[50] According to article 38 of the ICJ Statute,[51] the court shall follow and apply some defined sources to decide disputes in accordance with international law. These are also accepted as the sources of international law.

The Statue of International Court of Justice defines international custom as "evidence of a general practice accepted as law."[52] It can be said that milestones of the process of customary international law acquiring its contemporary basis of today are ICJ's North Sea Continental Shelf decision and the 1986 Nicaragua decision.[53] Although they have different aspects and dimensions, they defined and clarified the connections and relationship between two fundamental sources of international law, treaty, and tradition.[54] According to the ICJ's judgment on North Sea Continental Shelf case[55] for the creation of a customary international

---

48 Daniel Bodansky, "Non Liquet," *Max Planck Encyclopedia of Public International Law* (2006) opil.ouplaw.com/view/10.1093/law:epil/9780199231690/law-9780199231690-e1669?prd=EPIL (accessed 4 June 2018).

49 Akif Emre Öktem, *Uluslararası Teamül Hukuku*, İstanbul: Beta (2013), 511.

50 Ibid.

51 Statue of International Court of Justice, art. 38 www.icj-cij.org/documents/?p1=4&p2=2:

   a. international conventions, whether general or particular, establish rules expressly recognized by the contesting states;
   b. international custom, as evidence of a general practice accepted as law;
   c. the general principles of law recognized by civilized nations;
   d. subject to the provisions of Article 59, judicial decisions and the teachings of the most highly qualified publicists of the various nations, as subsidiary means for the determination of rules of law.

52 Ibid., art. 38 (1) (b).

53 ICJ, Military and Paramilitary Activities in and Against Nicaragua (*Nicaragua v. U.S.*) 1986.

54 Öktem, *Uluslararası Teamül*, 514.

55 North Sea Continental Shelf Case (*Germany v. Denmark*; *Germany v. Netherland*) (1969) 75 www.icj-cij.org/docket/files/52/5563.pdf.

law, there are two distinct elements: *state practice* and *opinio juris*. Similarly, in the *Libya/Malta* case, ICJ stated that founding elements of customary law are "actual practice and *opinio juris* of states."[56] While state practice should be general and consistent practice, *opinio juris* should be a "belief that a state activity is legally obligatory."[57]

Concerning the above requirements, while countries were signing the UN Charter at the San Francisco Conference, none of them believed that article 2 and article 51 included a prohibition on peacetime espionage activities.[58] Thus, there was not an *opinio juris* at that time, but there was *state practice* providing evidence for supporting and allowing peacetime intelligence-gathering activities. Nevertheless, the inclination towards regulating peacetime espionage activities became a dominant trend at the end of the Cold War.

The circumstances inherent to international relations and perceptions towards international law changed during the Cold War era. On one hand, states persisted in conducting peacetime espionage activities, however, on the other hand, states condemned other states which conducted espionage and looked for opportunities to retaliate. To illustrate, there was a general and persistent state practice for conducting reconnaissance flights in the so-called peacetime period during the Cold War. This period was dominated by countless reconnaissance flights conducted between competing powers. Whenever a reconnaissance flight was discovered, the targeted state always reacted against this activity, declared it as a violation of sovereignty and territorial integrity, and accused the other state of conducting espionage. Regarding the customary norm generation process of international law, *opinio juris* and *state practice* has evolved and developed for years in order to propose an international treaty. Having said that, the Treaty on Open Skies, which was signed in 1992 and put into effect in January 2002, established "the regime, to be known as the Open Skies regime, for the conduct of observation flights by States' Parties over the territories of other States' Parties."[59] This regime was designed as an instrument for confidence building between states. Pursuant to the treaty, 34

---

56 Case Concerning The Continental Shelf (*Libyan Arab Jamahiriya* v. *Malta*) (1985), 29 www.icj-cij.org/docket/files/68/6415.pdf (accessed 27 July 2015).
57 Malcolm N. Shaw, *International Law*, Cambridge: Cambridge University Press 6th edition (2008), 84; O. Elias, "The nature of the subjective element in customary international law," *ICLQ*, 44 (1995), 501.
58 John Yoo, "Counterintuitive: intelligence operations and international law," *MJIL*, 28 (2006), 628.
59 Treaty on Open Skies, art. 1/1 (entered into force 1 January 2002) http://disarmament. un.org/treaties/t/open_skies. Turkey is one of party states signed the Treaty at Helsinki on 24 March 1992.

signatory parties can conduct unarmed observation flights over entire territories of another state. It should be noted that this final document was an outcome of Cold War experiences, especially practices, incidents and allegations regarding reconnaissance flights between the US and Russia.

There are not any international law norms and principles, which explicitly or implicitly prohibited the espionage activities. There is an international custom on regulating specifically reconnaissance flights, not whole espionage activities. Although there is not any general principle of a law prohibiting espionage, espionage activities violate several of them. However, there are judicial decisions and the teachings of the most highly qualified scholars who accept espionage should be restricted as espionage violates several principles of international law.

PRINCIPLES OF INTERNATIONAL LAW AND ESPIONAGE

International legal scholars have reached a consensus on the fact that peacetime espionage activities violate the principle of territorial integrity, sovereign equality, non-intervention and peaceful cooperation of states. According to Wright, peacetime espionage operations are illegal according to principles "to respect the territorial integrity and political independence of other states" and such activities constitute an intervention, which "invades the territorial integrity and denies the political independence of another state."[60]

The Montevideo Convention[61] stipulates the definition and rights of statehood and has provisions on the principles of territorial integrity and non-intervention. According to article 8 of the Convention, "no state has the right to intervene in the internal or external affairs of another." Article 11 of the Convention states the principle of territorial integrity as "the territory of a state is inviolable and may not be the object of military occupation nor of other measures of force imposed by another state directly or indirectly or for any motive whatever even temporarily."

Article 4 of the Convention underlined the sovereign equality:

> States are juridically equal, enjoy the same rights, and have equal capacity in their exercise. The rights of each one do not depend upon the power which it possesses to assure its exercise, but upon the simple fact of its existence as a person under international law.

60 Wright, "Espionage and the doctrine of non-intervention in internal affairs," 4.
61 Montevideo Convention, signed December 26, 1933, entered into force on 26 December 1934, accessed http://avalon.law.yale.edu/20th_century/intam03.asp.

The Montevideo Convention set out those principles as a right of and responsibility upon every state that should be respected and acted on accordingly. The Charter of the United Nations has similar provisions. Article 2 of the Charter[62] states that the Organization is based on the principle of sovereign equality and all members shall refrain in their international relations from the threat or use of force against the territorial integrity or political independence of any state, or in any other manner inconsistent with the Purposes of the United Nations.

According to Kindred et al.,

> the dual concepts of sovereignty and equality are the cornerstone of public international law. Being sovereign and equal to others, a state has certain rights and corresponding duties. The rights include exclusive control over its territory, its permanent population [...] and other aspects of its domestic affairs. The necessary corollary is that there is a duty not to intervene overtly or covertly in the affairs of other states and thus not to interfere with their exclusive domestic jurisdiction.[63]

---

62 The Organization and its Members, in pursuit of the Purposes stated in Article 1 [Purposes of the United Nations], shall act in accordance with the following Principles.

1. The Organization is based on the principle of sovereign equality of all its Members.
2. All Members, in order to ensure all of them the rights and benefits resulting from membership, shall fulfill in good faith the obligations assumed by them in accordance with the present Charter.
3. All Members shall settle their international disputes by peaceful means in such a manner that international peace and security, and justice, are not endangered.
4. All Members shall refrain in their international relations from the threat or use of force against the territorial integrity or political independence of any state, or in any other manner inconsistent with the Purposes of the United Nations.
5. All Members shall give the United Nations every assistance in any action it takes in accordance with the present Charter, and shall refrain from giving assistance to any state against which the United Nations is taking preventive or enforcement action.
6. The Organization shall ensure that states which are not Members of the United Nations act in accordance with these Principles so far as may be necessary for the maintenance of international peace and security.
7. Nothing contained in the present Charter shall authorize the United Nations to intervene in matters which are essentially within the domestic jurisdiction of any state or shall require the Members to submit such matters to settlement under the present Charter; but this principle shall not prejudice the application of enforcement measures under Chapter VII.

63 H. M. Kindred et al., *International Law, Chiefly as Interpreted and Applied in Canada*, 5th ed., Toronto: Emond Publishing (1993), 16.

Similarly, Jonathan and Kovar stated that "l'espionnage fait appel à des moyens qui en eux-mêmes constituent des actes contraires au droit international."[64] In other words, peacetime espionage activities violate international law because such espionage uses means or tools which themselves constitute acts contrary to international law. Additionally, it is acknowledged by Wright that "in time of peace, however, espionage and, in fact, any penetration of the territory of a state by agents of another state in violation of the local law. It is also a violation of the rule of international law imposing a duty upon states to respect the territorial integrity and political independence of other states."[65]

In 2007, the Canadian Federal Court issued an exceptionally restrictive decision on cross-border intelligence activities. The Canadian Security Intelligence Service applied to the federal court for a warrant relating to investigative activities outside Canada pursuant to the Canadian Security Intelligence Service Act. The federal court interpreted domestic law in the light of international law norms and principles. Therefore, the federal court ruled

binding customary principles of international law, which prohibit interference with the sovereignty and domestic affairs of other states. The intrusive activities clearly impinge upon the above-mentioned principles of territorial sovereign equality and non-intervention and are likely to violate the laws of the jurisdiction where the investigative activities are to occur. By authorizing such activities, the warrant would, therefore, be authorizing activities that are inconsistent with and likely to breach the binding customary principles of territorial sovereign equality and non-intervention, by the comity of nations. These prohibitive rules of customary international law have evolved to protect the sovereignty of nation states against interference from other states. Extraterritorial jurisdiction, prescriptive, enforcement or adjudicative, exists under international law and is subject to the strict limits under international law based on sovereign equality, non-intervention, and the territorial principle.[66]

---

64 Gérard Cohen-Jonathan and Robert Kovar, "l'espionnage en Temps de Paix," *AFDIA*, 6(1) (1960), 246.
65 Wright, "Espionage and the doctrine of non-intervention in internal affairs," 12.
66 Canadian Federal Court, Canadian Security Intelligence Service Act (Re) (F.C.), 2008 FC 301 [2008] 4 F.C.R. 230 http://reports.fja-cmf.gc.ca/eng/2008/2008fc301.pdf (accessed 22 June 2015).

Violation of the above-mentioned principles of international law constitutes a base for the international responsibility of states. This responsibility is clearly stated by the United Nations General Assembly, as "states are internationally responsible for the activities of their intelligence services and agents, and any private contractors they engage, regardless of where these activities take place and who the victim of internationally wrongful conduct is."[67] Additionally, the Montreux document extends this responsibility to private contractors that perform intelligence functions on behalf of states.[68]

In this sense, from the 1945 signing of the UN Treaty to the end of the Cold War in 1990, states have chosen diplomatic, economical and sometimes military responses to peacetime espionage activities. The Open Skies Treaty is a good example of when states prefer regulated and foreknown activities. Alternatively, the Canadian Federal Court has underlined principles, founded in the Montevideo Convention and UN Charter, which may be used as a legal basis for the illegality of peacetime espionage activities. Therefore, peacetime espionage activities can simply constitute an international responsibility of attacker states.

Espionage and cyberespionage

Defining cyberespionage

The *Oxford Dictionary* defines cyberespionage as the use of computer networks to gain illicit access to confidential information, typically information held by a government or other organization.[69] The Tallinn Manual, under rule 66, defines cyberespionage narrowly as "any act undertaken clandestinely or under false pretenses that use of cyber capabilities to gather or attempt to gather information with the intention of communicating it to the opposing party and that act must occur in a territory controlled by a party to the conflict."[70] According to the UK Parliament, cyberespionage comprises cyber attacks that "have aimed to steal sensitive information and data from financial, government and

---

67 UNGA, Report of the Special Rapporteur on the promotion and protection of human rights and fundamental freedoms while countering terrorism A/HRC/14/46, 13 www2. ohchr.org/english/bodies/hrcouncil/docs/14session/A.HRC.14.46.pdf (accessed 4 June 2018).

68 ICRC, The Montreux Document on Private Military and Security Companies (2009), 12, 35.

69 *Oxford English Dictionary*, Oxford: Oxford University Press, 7 (2013), 234.

70 Michael N. Schmitt (ed.), *Tallinn Manual on the International Law Applicable to Cyber Warfare*, Cambridge: Cambridge University Press (2013), 158.

utilities infrastructure targets."[71] Similarly, Cyber Security Strategy documents of Germany state, "cyber attacks directed against the confidentiality of an IT system, which is launched or managed by foreign intelligence services, are called cyberespionage."[72] These attacks can target intellectual property or sensitive/secret information about organizations or governments.

Technically speaking, within this research, computer network operations (CNO) are defined as an umbrella term, which consists of computer network attacks (CNA), computer network defense (CND) and computer network exploitation (CNE). Definitions given in the Dictionary of Military and Associated Terms are adopted within this research.[73] According to the Dictionary, CNA or cyber attack refers to "actions taken via computer networks to disrupt, deny, degrade, or destroy information residing in computers and computer networks, or the computers and networks themselves."[74] CND refers to "actions to protect information systems and computer networks, and to monitor for, analyze, detect, and respond to unauthorized activity within those networks."[75] CNE concerns "actions to gather data from target information systems or networks or map target networks for future CNA operations."[76]

Hereinafter, cyberespionage will be used in the context of CNE. In other words, CNE "refers to operations conducted through the use of computer networks to gather data from targets or adversary automated information systems or networks."[77] It is also defined as cyber exploitation, "a term that refers to the penetration of adversary computers and networks to obtain information for intelligence purposes."[78] The International Group of Experts distinguished cyberespionage from CNE and cyber reconnaissance regarding its theater of operations. While CNE occurs from beyond enemy territory, cyberespionage is conducted within enemy territory. However, such distinction is not

---

71   UK Houses of Parliament, Cyber Security in the UK (2011), 2.
72   Federal Ministry of Interior, "Cyber security strategy for Germany" (2011), 14.
73   US Department of Defense, Dictionary of Military and Associated Terms, joint publications 1–02, 12 April 2001 (as amended through 26 August 2008), 113.
74   Ibid.
75   Ibid.
76   Ibid.
77   William A. Owens, Kenneth W. Dam and Herbert S. Lin (eds), *Technology, Policy, Law, and Ethics Regarding U.S. Acquisition and Use of Cyberattack Capabilities*, Washington, DC: National Academy Press (2009), 161.
78   Ibid., s. ix.

practical, because technically, it is difficult to make such a distinction and it is easier to conduct such activities beyond enemy territory without jeopardizing any individual likewise espionage activities. Second, traditionally defined legal consequences attached to spies who are operating within enemy territory cannot be applicable to personnel conducting cyber exploitation or cyberespionage from beyond enemy territory. Therefore, at the end of this chapter, it will become obvious that there is no technical difference between CNE and cyberespionage; it is only a terminological difference and there is no need for such a differentiation.

Legally speaking, cyberespionage operations are a kind of cyber attack, which targets commercial assets and trade secrets and provides unauthorized access to computers and networks. Therefore, those operations are punishable by criminal, civil, and administrative laws, as they constitute a wrongful acquisition of information, and unauthorized access to computer systems.

Changing features of espionage

From the Cold War period to today, the purposes, targets, actors of espionage and the methods applied for espionage have fundamentally transformed.[79] Targets of espionage activities have changed from military to economic and industrial secrets to gain an economic advantage over other states. Similarly, espionage activities are no longer conducted only by states and states' entities, but by a proliferation of, especially, civilian actors. Finally, the methods and means for gathering intelligence have shifted from human intelligence to signal intelligence.

Additionally, cyberspace has become a theater of conflicts and attacks between states. According to a report presented to the French Senate, "*à l'Internet est devenue facteur de vulnérabilité, si bien que*

---

79 Bruce Schneier, *Data and Goliath: The Hidden Battles to Collect Your Data and Control Your World*, New York: W. W. Norton & Company (2016), 55; "Electronic espionage is different today from what it was in the pre-Internet days of the Cold War. Before the Internet, when surveillance consisted largely of government to government espionage, agencies like the NSA would target specific communications circuits: that Soviet undersea cable between Petropavlovsk and Vladivostok, a military communications satellite, a microwave network. This was for the most part passive, requiring large antenna farms in nearby countries. Modern targeted surveillance is likely to involve actively breaking into an adversary's computer network and installing malicious software designed to take over that network and 'exfiltrate' data – that's NSA talk for stealing it. To put it more plainly, the easiest way for someone to eavesdrop on your communications isn't to intercept them in transit anymore; it's to hack your computer."

le réseau est maintenant le théâtre de véritables attaques qui peuvent provenir d'États, d'organisations ou même d'individus : espionnage économique, déstabilisation, sabotage d'infrastructures critiques.[80] In other words, the Internet has become a vulnerable factor, so that the network is now the scene of real attacks such as economic espionage, destabilization and sabotage to critical infrastructure that can come from states, organizations or individuals. Therefore, it is acknowledged that dual-use of the Internet and deployment of technology on espionage activities has accelerated because of the abovementioned change or shift.

New purposes and targets

For centuries, espionage activities have been conducted to gain military advantage. Spies infiltrated an army to disclose military secrets, collect information about size, capacity, and weapons, reveal military plans, and sometimes tempt soldiers to revolt. Nowadays, although espionage activities with the purpose of gaining military advantage are still conducted, economic and industrial espionage activities have reached a wider scope of applications.

Rapid development in the areas of communication services and computer technologies, and digitalization of vast pieces of information, have caused the proliferation of economic and industrial espionage activities. Furthermore, not only are state-owned critical infrastructures and networks increasingly being targeted and becoming vulnerable to state-backed economic cyberespionage operations, but also private networks and company databases.[81] In 2009, a UK government security document revealed the shift in intelligence-gathering operations and targets:

> In the past, espionage activity was typically directed towards obtaining political and military intelligence. In today's high-tech world, the intelligence requirements of a number of countries now include new communications technologies, IT, genetics, aviation,

80 Catherine Morin-Desailly, *Rapport D'information fait au nom de la mission commune d'information nouveau rôle et nouvelle stratégie pour l'Union européenne dans la gouvernance mondiale de l'Internet* (8 July 2014), Rapports Parlementaires No.: 696, 307 www.senat.fr/rap/r13-696-1/r13-696-11.pdf (accessed 4 June 2018).
81 Craig Mundie, Speaking on the Future of Technology Conference Columbia University School of International and Public Affairs (8 November 2013) www.youtube.com/watch?v=tnojfzVv7eA (accessed 22 June 2015).

Table 1.1 China-based APT groups targeting of strategic emerging industries

Strategic emerging industry	Number of China-based APT groups targeting this strategic emerging industry
Clean energy technology	3
Next-generation IT	19
Biotechnology	6
High-end equipment manufacturing	22
Alternative energy	7
New materials	12
New energy vehicles	6

lasers, optics, electronics and many other fields. Intelligence services, therefore, are targeting commercial enterprises far more than in the past.[82]

Thus, intelligence-gathering activities are nowadays more about collecting financial and economic data, and business secrets and plans. The trend is shifting from military to commercial espionage, and human intelligence to signal intelligence.

Similarly, during her testimony before the US.-China Economic and Security Review Commission, FireEye Threat Intelligence Department Manager Jen Weedon mentioned that foreign actors have targeted several strategic sectors in US (see Table 1.1).[83]

According to Weedon, along with the sectors mentioned above, electronics, telecommunications, robotics, data services, pharmaceuticals, mobile phone services, satellite communications and imagery and business application software-based sectors were also being targeted.[84] It is significant to collect highly sensitive and valuable information, but what is more significant is to apply them properly in the market and

82 Sean Rayment, "Britain under attack from 20 foreign spy agencies including France and Germany," *The Telegraph* (7 February 2009) www.telegraph.co.uk/news/uknews/defence/4548753/Britain-under-attack-from-20-foreign-spy-agencies-including-France-and-Germany.html (accessed 22 June 2015).
83 US-China Economic and Security Review Commission, Hearing on Commercial Cyber Espionage and Barriers to Digital Trade in China, testimony of Jen Weedon (2015), 4 www.uscc.gov/sites/default/files/Weedon%20Testimony.pdf.
84 Ibid., s. 4–8.

industry. In particular, economic espionage has several stages from collection to innovation. The model of espionage effectiveness provides a comprehensive illustration of those stages.[85] Collected information and data has to be analyzed and categorized in accordance with domestic requirements and needs. At a later stage, the industry will adopt those outputs and produce new products. These products will enable the domestic sector and products to gain competitive advantages in the international market against other domestic markets and similar products.

Therefore, the focal point of economic cyberespionage activities and security technologies becomes company data, which includes personal data, confidential data and intellectual property.

New methods and means

The intelligence-gathering methods and means have radically changed in the last two decades. States have always been in pursuit of adopting new approaches and improving their electronic capabilities to collect better information from targeted states. Throughout the 1990s and early 2000s, the first phase of cyber attacks (such as DDOS), and malware such as viruses, worms, and Trojan horses, were commonly applied. Later, there was the creation of tailored cyber weapons. According to Rid and McBurney, a cyber weapon is "a computer code that is used, or designed to be used, with the aim of threatening or causing physical, functional, or mental harm to structures, systems, or living beings."[86]

The Stuxnet is the first-known malicious computer worm tailored to target specific platforms such as PLC's (programmable logic controllers) and SCADA (supervisory control and data acquisition) systems. Stuxnet is a "cyber weapon created and deployed with the intent of degrading, disrupting, and destroying a specific information system."[87] This malware was designed to collect information on the industrial systems of Iranian nuclear facilities, including either the Bushehr Nuclear Power Plant or the Natanz nuclear facility, and it caused the

---

85 Jon R. Lindsay, Tai Ming Cheung and Derek S. Reveron (eds), *China and Cybersecurity: Espionage, Strategy, and Politics in the Digital Domain*, Oxford: Oxford University Press (2015), 54.

86 Thomas Rid and Peter McBurney, "Cyber-weapons," *RUSI Journal*, 157(1) (2012), 7; Thomas Rid, *Cyber War Will Not Take Place*, Oxford: Oxford University Press (2013), 37.

87 Emilio Iasiello, "Are cyber weapons effective military tools?," *Military and Strategic Affairs*, 7(1) (2015), 32.

fast-spinning centrifuges to tear themselves apart within the targeted uranium enrichment facility at Natanz. Three other major espionage tools have also been discovered that seem to link to Stuxnet. The pioneer of cyberespionage toolkits, Gauss, discovered in 2012, was designed to be a complex cyber weapon, which steals passwords and other data. The second was Flame, which is able to take over drivers, screenshots, Skype, and Bluetooth functions, and can monitor a computer's keyboard and network traffic. The third toolkit was the DuQu, which operates in the background and collects data for years.

APT is one of the most significant cyber weapons, applied commonly for conducting cyberespionage operations.[88] It is a sophisticated technique used by hackers to extract large amounts of data from targeted industries over a long period.[89] According to Cole, key terms that describe the APT are "stealthy, targeted, adaptive and data focused."[90] This type of attack is well-tailored to the targeted sector or computer networks and it has advanced capabilities to extract data and compromise the targeted entity. Such an adversary can spend years infiltrating the documents of a targeted entity without being spotted. According to the recent white paper published by McAfee, "APT differs from common botnets and malware type attacks because they target strategic users to gain undetected access to key assets."[91]

Throughout the history of espionage, none of the states accepted regulating and restricting the use of tools and means of espionage activities. However, nowadays, commonly used tools and means for espionage activities have dual-use characteristics. These tools and means can be used to either protect citizens and digital assets or target individuals and steal digital assets and trade secrets. For instance, the Wassenaar Arrangement on Export Controls for Conventional Arms and Dual-Use

---

88 Paul Taylor, "Industrial espionage cyber style," *Financial Times* (8 November 2011): "Generally the term is used to designate a cybercrime category directed at business and political targets. Typically APTs require a high degree of stealthiness and the attack takes place over a prolonged period of time. Often they appear motivated by factors beyond immediate financial gain, and compromised systems continue to be of service even after key systems have been breached and initial goals reached. More often than not, the target organization is unaware of the attack until alerted by a third party."

89 Mandiant, "APT1: exposing one of China's cyber espionage units," February 2013 www.fireeye.com/content/dam/fireeye-www/services/pdfs/mandiant-apt1-report.pdf (accessed 4 June 2018).

90 Eric Cole, *Advanced Persistent Threat: Understanding the Danger and How to Protect Your Organization*, Waltham: Elsevier (2013), 20–21.

91 McAfee, Combating Advanced Persistent Threats: How to prevent, detect, and remediate APTs, White Papers (2011) www.mcafee.com/us/resources/white-papers/wp-combat-advanced-persist-threats.pdf.

Goods and Technologies[92] is an international agreement designed to control the export of dual-use technologies. The agreement creates a special regime for controlling and regulating the export of guns, landmines and other weapons and their components. In December 2013, the list of controlled technologies was amended to include intrusion and surveillance items. According to the Wassenaar Arrangement, "intrusion software" is defined as software specially designed or modified to avoid detection by "monitoring tools," or to defeat "protective countermeasures," of a computer or network capable device, and performing a. the extraction of data or information, from a computer or network capable device, or the modification of system or user data; or b. the modification of the standard execution path of a program or process in order to allow the execution of externally provided instructions.[93]

Although the agreement is not legally binding and signatory countries should implement the changes in the agreement into their domestic legal systems, 31 of 41 countries have implemented the changes. Some

92 The Wassenaar Arrangement on Export Controls for Conventional Arms and Dual-Use Goods and Technologies, accepted on 11–12 July 1996, www.wassenaar.org/app/uploads/2018/01/WA-DOC-17-PUB-006-Public-Docs-Vol.II-2017-List-of-DU-Goods-and-Technologies-and-Munitions-List.pdf.

93 The scope of restrictions has been widened with recent amendments and the categories listed below become subject to export control:

4. A. 5. Systems, equipment, and components therefore, specially designed or modified for the generation, operation or delivery of, or communication with, "intrusion software".

4. D. 4. "Software" specially designed or modified for the generation, operation or delivery of, or communication with, "intrusion software".

4. E. 1. c "Technology" for the "development" of "intrusion software".

4. D. 1. a "Software" specially designed or modified for the "development" or "production" of equipment or "software" specified by 4.A. or 4.D.

4. E. 1 "Technology" according to the General Technology Note, for the "development", "production" or "use" of equipment or "software" specified by 4.A. or 4.D.
IP network surveillance systems
5. A. 1. j. IP network communications surveillance systems or equipment, and specially designed components therefore, having all of the following:

> *1. Performing all of the following on a carrier class IP network (e.g., national grade IP backbone):*
>> *a. Analysis at the application layer (e.g., Layer 7 of Open Systems Interconnection (OSI) model (ISO/IEC 7498-1));*
>> *b. Extraction of selected metadata and application content (e.g., voice, video, messages, attachments); and*
>> *c. Indexing of extracted data; and*
> *2. Being specially designed to carry out all of the following:*
>> *a. Execution of searches on the basis of "hard selectors"; and*
>> *b. Mapping of the relational network of an individual or of a group of people.*

scholars argued that this would hamper the efforts of oppressive regimes to monitor and profile their citizens. Other scholars opposed the changes that cover tools, which enable states to improve their cyber security level.[94] In any case, it reflects a tendency towards regulating cyber intrusion tools and later cyberespionage.

New actors and incidents

Every state has authorized intelligent authorities and laws regulating foreign intelligence gathering.[95] In this regard, every state is trying to maintain an optimum balance between national security needs and effective functioning of law enforcement authorities on the one hand, and right to privacy and Personal Data Protection on the other. As the right to privacy and Personal Data Protection begins to be accepted as a part of international human rights, this existing balance has needed to be reconsidered and tailored not only by taking into account citizens but also international society and citizens of other states. Invasive application of technologies and concerns are related to this, paving the way for several high courts, such as the US Supreme Court and Canadian Supreme Court, to decide on restricting further the activities of foreign intelligence gathering. However, it is important to note that the very foundation of that decision is to protect the basic rights of citizens and respect for international rules and principles.

> *ML11. Electronic equipment, "spacecraft" and components, not specified elsewhere on the Munitions List, as follows:*
> > *a. Electronic equipment specially designed for military use and specially designed components therefore;*
> *Note ML11.a. includes:*
> > *c. Electronic systems or equipment, designed either for surveillance and monitoring of the electromagnetic spectrum for military intelligence or security purposes or for counteracting such surveillance and monitoring;*
> > *i. Digital demodulators specially designed for signals intelligence;*

94 European Commission, Cybersecurity Strategy of the European Union: An Open, Safe and Secure Cyberspace, 52013JC0001 (2013), "Cyber-security commonly refers to the safeguards and actions that can be used to protect the cyber domain, both in the civilian and military fields, from those threats that are associated with or that may harm its interdependent networks and information infrastructure. Cyber security strives to preserve the availability and integrity of the networks and infrastructure and the confidentiality of the information contained therein."

95 This report contains information on laws regulating the collection of intelligence in the European Union and selected European Union (EU) Member States, see Peter Roudik, *Foreign Intelligence Gathering Laws*, Washington, DC: The Law Library of Congress (December 2014) www.loc.gov/law/help/foreign-intelligence-gathering/foreign-intelligence-gathering.pdf (accessed 4 June 2018).

Table 1.2 Top trending cyberespionage actors in 2016

Group 27	Gaza Hacker Team
Scarlet Mimic	SandWorm Team
Poseidon APT Group	Russian Intelligence Agency
Firas Dardar	Codosa Team
Pawn Storm	Ahmad Umar Agha
APT 28	Peter Romar
GCHQ	Lazarus Group
Suckfly Group	NSA

Along with perpetrators of organized crime, hired-hand attackers,[96] as well as industrial competitors or hacker groups such as Anonymous or RedHack, cyberespionage attacks can come from national intelligence services.[97] SurfWatch Labs revealed the top trending cyberespionage actors in 2016. "Group 27, which is a cyberespionage group linked with the Seven Pointed Dagger malware campaign that utilizes a remote access Trojan known as Trochilus, is the top trending espionage actor in 2016."[98] There are also governmental agencies included in the list, such as the NSA, GCHQ, and Russian Intelligence Agency. However, it is significant to clarify that cyberespionage operations conducted by private actors fall under the scope of this research if they might be attributed to a state, or state organs knowingly aiding and abetting those groups, or the government of the state where the threat is located within their territory and they are unwilling or unable to prevent the use of its territory for such attacks.

It is acknowledged that the activities of intelligent services are far more capable than other actors. This is not to say that the incidents and operations mentioned here do not point a finger or accuse any nation and its officials. These incidents are strong proof that states can perform such activities, although they are irritated at being targeted.[99] However,

96 James Sperling (ed.) *Handbook of Governance and Security*, Cheltenham: Edward Elgar Publishing (2014), 343.
97 Ellen Messmer, "Cyber-espionage attacks threaten corporate data in new unrelenting ways," Network World (2011) www.networkworld.com/article/2179877/security/cyberespionage- attacks-threaten-corporate-data-in-new-unrelenting-ways.html (accessed 22 June 2015).
98 Matt Lichtfuss, "Cyber-espionage making headlines over past couple weeks," SurfWatchLabs (2016) https://blog.surfwatchlabs.com/2016/06/16/cyber-espionage-making-headlines-over-past-couple-weeks/ (accessed 4 June 2018).
99 See for some cases of industrial espionage and/or competitive intelligence which have been described in the press or in the relevant literature: EU Parliament, Report on

the aim is to show the fact that cyberespionage activities are commonly deployed, supported or backed both by official and private actors. As acknowledged in the *Tallinn Manual*: "the mere fact that a cyber operation has been launched or otherwise originates from governmental cyber infrastructure is not sufficient evidence for attributing the operation to that state, but it is an indication that the state in question is associated with the operation."[100] The following section highlights some of the significant cyberespionage operations as proof that there is a state practice and willingness to regulate this area. Additionally, cyberespionage operations organized by a state's organs (agencies, institutions) and private actors should be treated separately because both have different legal consequences and should be addressed by different legal mechanisms.

PRIVATE ACTORS

In 2009, scholars from the University of Toronto and University of Cambridge published a report revealing field-based research and findings of the malware-based cyberespionage network, GhostNet.[101] According to the findings, this malware-based cyberespionage network infiltrated 1,295 computers in 103 countries. Scholars underlined that "up to 30 percent of the infected computers are considered high-value targets and include computers located at ministries of foreign affairs, embassies, international organizations, news media, and NGOs."[102] In 2010, David Drummond, Google's Corporate Development and Chief Legal Officer, explained that highly sophisticated attacks, labeled "Operation Aurora" by McAfee, targeted the Google infrastructure from China to infiltrate its corporate properties.[103] However, this attack not only targeted Google. The Google investigation team discovered that at least 20 large companies including Yahoo, Symantec, Adobe, Northrop Grumman and Dow Chemical had also been among the targets.[104]

the Existence of A Global System for the Interception of Private and Commercial Communications (ECHELON interception system) (2001/2098(INI)).

100 Schmitt, *Tallinn Manual*, 34.

101 Ron Deibert and Rafal Rohozinski, "Tracking GhostNet: investigating a cyber espionage network," University of Toronto, Munk Centre for International Studies at Trinity College (2009) www.nsi.org/pdf/reports/Cyber%20Espionage%20Network.pdf (accessed 22 June 2015).

102 Ibid., 40.

103 David Drummond, "A new approach to China" (12 January 2010) http://googleblog.blogspot.co.uk/2010/01/new-approach-to-china.html (accessed 25 June 2015).

104 Ariana Eunjung Cha and Ellen Nakashima, "Google China cyberattack part of vast espionage campaign, experts say," *Washington Post* (14 January 2010) www.washingtonpost.com/wp-dyn/content/article/2010/01/13/AR2010011300359.html (accessed 25 June 2015).

Technically named advanced persistent threats (APT) are gaining access to privileged systems and maintaining their access until they are disclosed. GhostNet and Operation Aurora were both designed as APTs. Along with GhostNet and Operation Aurora, in 2011, McAfee attributed a cyber attack to China's government, named "Night Dragon," and stated in a report that attackers had exfiltrated computer systems of global oil, energy and petrochemical companies.[105] The "Night Dragon" attack caused the companies a loss of "proprietary operations and project-financing information that can make or break multibillion dollar deals."[106]

Although the activities mentioned above have attribution problems, because those are private groups, a report published by Mandiant in 2013 established the attribution link. According to the report, a special unit of the Chinese People's Liberation Army (PLA) was targeting financial and industrial companies for large-scale theft of intellectual property or industrial and economic espionage. The report underlined the fact that APT malware has been active since 2006, and compromises 141 companies in 20 major industries.[107] Table 1.3 illustrates other APT-type attacks which are supposed to have originated from China.

In 2015, several research companies working on cyber intelligence revealed that China-based cyber actors have carried out intrusion activities on targets across Southeast Asia, including ASEAN. ThreatConnect, in partnership with Defense Group Inc., published another report that "has attributed the targeted cyberespionage infrastructure activity associated with the Naikon APT group to a specific unit of the PLA."[108] It was further stated: "Unit 78020 conducts cyberespionage against Southeast Asian military, diplomatic, and economic targets. The targets

---

105 McAfee, "Global energy cyberattacks: 'Night Dragon'" (10 February 2011) www. mcafee.com/uk/resources/white-papers/wp-global-energy-cyberattacks-night-dragon.pdf (accessed 25 June 2015).

106 Georger Kurtz, McAfee, "Global energy cyberattacks: 'Night Dragon,'" 10 Feburary 2011 https://blogs.mcafee.com/business/global-energy-industry-hit-in-night-dragon-attacks/; McAfee, "Global energy cyberattacks: 'Night Dragon,'" Report 2011, https://ics-cert.us-cert.gov/advisories/ICSA-11-041-01A.

107 Mandiant, "APT1 exposing one of China's cyber espionage units" (18 February 2013) http://intelreport.mandiant.com/Mandiant_APT1_Report.pdf (accessed 25 June 2015).

108 ThreatConnect and Defense Group Inc., "Project Camerashy: closing the aperture on China's unit 78020" ThreatConnect (2015) www.threatconnect.com/camerashy/ (accessed 4 June 2018). According to the report, "Naikon is known as affiliated with PLA Unit 78020, the Second Technical Reconnaissance Bureau under the Chengdu Military Region."

Table 1.3 Publicly reported cyberespionage activities attributed to China

Name of attack	Date identified	Target	Source of attack
Nitro	2011	50 companies, including 29 chemical firms and 19 firms mostly in the defense industry; Fortune 100 companies that conduct chemical compound R&D	Symantec identifies author of the attacks and attributes the patterns of attacks to Chinese hackers. Attack traced back to single hacker in Hebei province
Operation Beebus	2011	The set of targets cover all aspects of unmanned vehicles, land, air, and sea, from research to design to manufacturing of the vehicles and their various subsystems	FireEye Labs has linked the attacks to the China-based Comment Group hacker collective (a prolific actor believed to be affiliated with the Chinese government)
Operation Aurora	2009–2010	Adobe Systems, Juniper Networks and Rackspace publicly confirmed that they were targeted. According to media reports, Yahoo, Symantec, Northrop Grumman, Morgan Stanley and Dow Chemical were also among the targets	Series of cyber attacks conducted by a group based in Beijing, China, with ties to the People's Liberation Army. First publicly disclosed by Google on January 12, 2010, in a blogpost
Night Dragon	2009–2011	Multinational firms in the oil/energy sector (sensitive internal documents, including proprietary information about oil- and gas-field operations, project financing and bidding documents)	Originated from China according to McAfee

(continued)

Table 1.3 (Cont.)

Name of attack	Date identified	Target	Source of attack
RSA	2010	RSA, Lockheed	Compromise of industry standard RSA SecureID tokens enabled Lockheed intrusion
F-35 JSF	2007–2009	BAE, Lockheed-Martin, Northrop Grumman	APT compromised non-classified data on F-25, monitored meetings and technical discussions
Telvent	2007	Telvent/Schneider Electric: Telvent said the attacker(s) installed malicious software and stole project files related to one of its core offerings – OASyS SCADA – a product that helps energy firms mesh older IT assets with more advanced "smart grid" technologies.	Attributed to China-based Comment Group
QinetiQ	2007	QinetiQ North America (NA) is a world-leading defense technology and security company that provides technological equipment such as satellites, drones and software services to the US Special Forces	Chinese hackers belonging to Comment Crew conducted an operation that started in 2009. Hackers compromised at least 151 machines of the company. The attacks lasted around 251 days during which they stole 20 gigabytes of data before being blocked
Titan Rain	2003–2006	10 most prominent US defense contractors–including Raytheon, Lockheed-Martin, Boeing and Northrop Grumman	Chinese military hackers (according to the SANS Institute)

include government entities in Cambodia, Indonesia, Laos, Malaysia, Myanmar, Nepal, the Philippines, Singapore, Thailand, and Vietnam as well as international bodies such as United Nations Development Program (UNDP) and ASEAN."[109] In 2017, Secureworks incident responders and Counter Threat Unit (CTU) researchers investigated activities associated with the Bronze Butler cyberespionage group.[110] They revealed that this private group has been targeting companies and organizations located in Japan. They were mostly top-heavy industry companies and critical infrastructures. Bronze Butler group was trying to infiltrate "intellectual property related to technology and developments, product specifications, sensitive business and sales-related information, network and system configuration files, e-mail messages and meeting minutes."[111]

AGENCIES OF STATES OR STATE-SPONSORED ACTORS

The revelations of Edward Snowden[112] regarding the NSA and other national intelligence services indicated that intelligence organizations are capable of collecting data through electronic means from around the world. The global reach of the Internet enables large-scale techniques of surveillance as well as bulk data collection and extraction. It became possible to harvest data from submarine Internet cables via different interceptors such as UPSTREAM and QUANTUMISERT.[113] However, this global data collection requires transnational collaboration, because the NSA cannot control the data totally, absolutely and globally by itself. The well-known structure for such collaboration is the Five Eyes

109 Ibid., 7 See also, Josh Chin, "Cyber sleuth track hacker to China's military," *The Wall Street Journal* (23 September 2015) www.wsj.com/articles/cyber-sleuths-track-hacker-to-chinas-military-1443042030 (accessed 4 June 2018).
110 Secureworks Counter Threat Unit Research Team, "BRONZE BUTLER targets Japanese enterprises" (12 October 2017) www.secureworks.com/research/bronze-butler-targets-japanese-businesses (accessed 20 December 2017); Council on Foreign Relations, Cyber Operations Tracker "Bronze Butler" www.cfr.org/interactive/cyber-operations/bronze-butler (accessed 20 December 2017): "This threat actor targets organizations in the critical infrastructure, heavy industry, manufacturing, and international relations sectors for espionage purposes."
111 Ibid.
112 Glenn Greenwald, Ewen MacAskill and Laura Poitras, "Edward Snowden: the whistleblower behind the NSA surveillance revelations," *Guardian* (11 June 2013) www.theguardian.com/world/2013/jun/09/edward-snowden-nsa-whistleblower-surveillance (accessed 22 June 2015).
113 Edward Snowden, UPSTREAM and QUANTUMISERT see more: https://search.edwardsnowden.com.

Alliance, 9-Eyes, and 14-Eyes programs.[114] The Five Eyes Alliance was set up by the UKUSA Agreement,[115] and authorized the United States National Security Agency (NSA), the United Kingdom's Government Communications Headquarters (GCHQ), the Communications Security Establishment Canada (CSEC), the Australian Signals Directorate (ASD) and New Zealand's Government Communications Security Bureau (GCSB) to collect and share signal intelligence.

The signing parties agreed to exchange the products of the following operations relating to foreign communication: a collection of traffic, acquisition of communication documents and equipment, traffic analysis, cryptanalysis, decryption and translation and acquisition of information regarding communication, organizations, practices, procedures and equipment.[116]

The NSA solely collects and analyzes data to hand over to national security agencies such as the CIA and FBI. The NSA was authorized to collect foreign intelligence due to national security concerns by the Foreign Intelligence Surveillance Act (FISA).[117] Revelations about the NSA indicated that the PRISM surveillance program was designed to collect e-mails, communications, texts and video chats of foreigners.[118] The main justifications or exceptions granted by law are 1) counter-terrorism, 2) organized crime and 3) national security interests.[119] Section 702 of the FISA provides a legal basis for the collection of "foreign intel information" regarding persons who are "reasonably believed to be located outside of the U.S."[120] Although the NSA's surveillance program, such as PRISM, ignited debate on privacy and data protection in the US related to human rights and protection mechanisms of the US Constitution, there were other programs like Blarney and Rampart-T that serve the purpose of traditional espionage targeting foreign

---

114 The 9-eyes program includes the US, UK, Canada, Australia, New Zealand, Denmark, France, Norway and the Netherlands; the 14-eyes program includes those countries and also Germany, Belgium, Italy, Spain and Sweden.
115 UKUSA Agreement (adopted on 10 May 1955) www.nsa.gov/public_info/declass/ukusa.shtml (accessed 22 June 2015).
116 UKUSA COMINT Agreement and Appendices Thereto (adopted 26 June 1951) www.nsa.gov/public_info/_files/ukusa/ukusa_comint_agree.pdf (accessed 22 June 2015).
117 Foreign Intelligence Surveillance Act 50 U.S.C. sec. 1881a http://fas.org/irp/news/2013/06/nsa-sect702.pdf (accessed 22 June 2015).
118 Barton Gellman and Laura Poitras, "U.S., British intelligence mining data from nine U.S. Internet companies in broad secret program," *Washington Post* (7 June 2013).
119 Oğuz Kaan Pehlivan, "İpin ucunu kaçırmak," *NSA, Analist Journal*, 34 (December 2013), 24–25.
120 Foreign Intelligence Surveillance Act 50 U.S.C. sec. 1881.

governments.[121] It was also revealed that through those programs the NSA could gain access to several diplomatic missions of the EU and the UN Headquarters in New York.[122] Apart from the international human rights concerns, the Vienna Convention on Diplomatic Relations protects diplomatic communications between capitals and missions whose norms are regarded as a custom accepted by all states. Article 27 of the Convention underlined that "the receiving State shall permit and protect free communication on the part of the mission for all official purposes."[123] In this regard, basic tapping into the communication of diplomatic premises constitutes a violation of international obligation.

Furthermore, alleged economic espionage activities of the NSA have been disclosed by documents showing that the computer networks of Petrobras, the semi-state-owned Brazilian oil company, have been targeted and exfiltrated. Similarly, the Minister of Economy of France, Philippe Lemoine, in his speech during the hearing at the French Senate stated that

> aux États-Unis, le contexte juridique, avec au premier chef le Patriot Act, s'est traduit, ainsi que le révèle le Washington Post, par une habilitation au secret-défense de 840 000 personnes, dont 135 000 seulement dans les agences de renseignement. Autrement dit, beaucoup sont dans les entreprises. Ces personnes ont deux employeurs, leur entreprise, et la NSA ... Dans cet important appareillage, une part, très visible, se concentre sur la lutte contre le terrorisme, mais la plus grande part, beaucoup moins visible, se voue à l'espionnage économique.[124]

Lemoine said that, according to information in the *Washington Post*, pursuant to the legal context created by the Patriot Act, only 135,000 personnel out of 840,000 have been working at intelligence agencies, but

121 Edward Snowden, RAMPART-A Project Overview https://search.edwardsnowden.com/docs/RAMPART-AProjectOverview20140618 (accessed 22 June 2015).
122 Laura Poitras, Marcel Rosenbach and Holger Stark, "Codename 'Apalachee': how America spies on Europe and the UN," *Der Spiegel* (26 August 2013) www.spiegel.de/international/world/secret-nsa-documents-show-how-the-us-spies-on-europe-and-the-un-a-918625.html (accessed 22 June 2015).
123 Vienna Convention on Diplomatic Relations (adopted 18 April 1961, entered into force 24 April 1964), 500 UNTS 95.
124 Ministère du Commerce et de l'Industrie, Comptes Rendus de la MCI sur la Gouvernance Mondiale De L'internet, speech of Philippe Lemoine, 24 March 2014, www.senat.fr/compte-rendu-commissions/20140324/mci_gouv.html (accessed 4 June 2018).

all 840,000 personnel have authorization to access state secrets. In other words, most of the personnel work at private companies. Those people have two employers: their company and the NSA. In this context, the visible part focuses on the fight against terrorism, but the other less visible part is dedicated to economic espionage.[125]

Nevertheless, Vanee Vines, an NSA spokesperson, denied any allegations of using foreign intelligence capabilities to "steal the trade secrets of foreign companies on behalf of U.S. companies to enhance their international competitiveness," but rather explained economic espionage based on national security.[126] Likewise, Mike Rogers, the chairperson of the House Intelligence Committee, denied economic espionage activities by the NSA and stated "economic espionage is against the law in the United States. If they [the NSA] do it, they are going to jail."[127] Despite the denials from US officials, Brazilian officials confirmed the interception and economic espionage activities of the NSA. H. E. Dilma Rousseff, former president of the Federative Republic of Brazil, underlined the industrial espionage activities targeting Petrobras in her speech at the opening of the general debate of the 68th session of the United Nations General Assembly. In her speech, Rousseff stated: "corporate information – often of high economic and even strategic value – was at the center of espionage activity," describing the activities as industrial espionage and "a breach of International Law."[128]

125 In his speech, Lemoine mentioned "visible and less visible parts" of NSA, there is not further explaination about the content and definition of those terms. However, he might be referring the NSA's public activities and covert/clandestine operations and activities.
126 James Glanz and Andrew W. Lehren, "NSA spied on allies, aid groups and businesses," *The New York Times* (20 December 2013) www.nytimes.com/2013/12/21/world/nsa-dragnet-included-allies-aid-groups-and-business-elite.html?_r=0 (accessed 23 July 2015).
127 Sam Jones, "U.S. spies engaged in industrial espionage will be jailed, says lawmaker," *Financial Times* (31 January 2014); Michael Rogers, "Panel discussion 'rebooting trust? freedom v. security in cyberspace'," Munich Security Conference (31 January to 2 February 2014) www.securityconference.de/media-library/videos/?tx_tvmediacenter_mediacenter%5Bcontroller%5D=Mediacenter&tx_tvmediacenter_mediacenter%5Bsearch_result%5D=320&cHash=b463f65bf1dae400bcd5f986133af1e0 (accessed 22 June 2015).
128 Statement by H. E. Dilma Rousseff, President of The Federative Republic of Brazil, at the opening of the general debate of the 68th session of the United Nations General Assembly (New York, 24 September 2013) http://gadebate.un.org/sites/default/files/gastatements/68/BR_en.pdf (accessed 22 July 2015).

States are held responsible for any kind of actions of their agencies and organs.[129] However, attribution problems occur when the cyberespionage has conducted by private actors. Likewise, if a targeted state could not identify the attacker, but identify only their location, then again such actions have to be attributed to the host state which needs to be held liable for the consequences of such actions. To establish that attribution link, the host state should be aware of the attackers and their activities, but do not want interfere to prevent such actions or simply are not able to do so. There are ongoing discussions and speculations regarding the attribution problem. Attribution is about finding responsible individuals and entities then having reasonable clues to establish a causal link between perpetrators and state organs or governments. Therefore, it becomes possible to attribute illegal cyber activities to a government or state and label those activities as "state-sponsored, backed or financed." However, the problem of attribution and the methods applied for attributing any cyber activity to officials is outwith the scope of this research. We have instead focused on illustrating the fact that states are conducting economic cyberespionage activities and trying to find and adopt counter measures in which all attacking and defending activities provide a basis for state practice.

Unlike human-based intelligence-gathering operations, signal-based intelligence-gathering activities can be conducted covertly and without risk of being detected for a long time. Moreover, attributing any kind of cyber operations to states or state officials and bodies is a complex process, because proving the link between them is both technically and legally challenging. Detecting the source of an attack does not automatically provide a link between operations or support of a state. According to the Tallinn Manual Rule 7: "the mere fact that a cyber operation has been launched or otherwise originates from governmental cyber infrastructure is not sufficient evidence for attributing the operations to that

---

129 Article 4 of the Responsibility of States for Internationally Wrongful Acts, 2001, *Yearbook of the International Law Commission*, 2(2) (2001) http://legal.un.org/ilc/texts/instruments/english/draft_articles/9_6_2001.pdf (4 June 2018).

   1. The conduct of any State organ shall be considered an act of that State under international law, whether the organ exercises legislative, executive, judicial or any other functions, whatever position it holds in the organization of the State, and whatever its character as an organ of the central Government or of a territorial unit of the State.
   2. An organ includes any person or entity which has status in accordance with the internal law of the State.

State but is an indication that the State in question is associated with the operation."[130] According to Roscini, "official state documents, such as national legislation, cyber doctrines, manuals, strategies, directives, and rules of engagement, may become relevant in establishing state responsibility for cyber operations."[131] This shows that actors are targeting both public and private networks for economic espionage purposes. Therefore, a targeted state can apply certain legal mechanisms to tackle these operations.

To this end, founding features of espionage activities have changed and states can be both the victim and perpetrator of economic cyberespionage activities. Regarding the above-mentioned explanations, economic espionage activities to gain strategic advantage have proliferated. There are several reasons for such a proliferation: first, the costs and externalities are low compared to traditional espionage. To illustrate this, according to the BLACKOPS Partners Corporation, which focuses on counterintelligence and protection of trade secrets for Fortune 500 companies, 500 billion USD in raw innovation is stolen from US companies each year.[132] "Raw innovation includes trade secrets, research and development, and products that give companies a competitive advantage."[133] Casey Fleming, CEO of BLACKOPS Partners Corporation, explains: "when this innovation is meant to drive revenue, profit, and jobs for at least 10 years, we are losing the equivalent of 5 trillion dollars out of the U.S. economy every year to economic espionage. To put it into perspective, the U.S. will take in 1.5 trillion dollars in income taxes and 2.7 trillion dollars in all taxes in 2013."[134]

Second, determining the origin and attributing the attack to officials is difficult and complicated. Third, it may take years to spot and detect cyberespionage activities, especially APT-type attacks. Finally, there is an underdeveloped legal framework to decide appropriate responses. Therefore, in order to respond to this change effectively and legally and

---

130 Schmitt, *Tallinn Manual*, 39.
131 Marco Roscini, "Evidentiary issues in international disputes related to state responsibility for cyber operations," *Texas International Law Journal*, 50(2) (2015), 256; Mark D. Young, "National cyber doctrine: the missing link in the application of American cyber power," *Journal of National Security Law & Policy* 173 (2010), 175–76.
132 For more information BLACKOPS Partners, visit https://blackopspartners.com/firm/ (accessed 4 June 2018).
133 Joshua Philipp, "The staggering cost of economic espionage against the US," *Epoch Times* (22 October 2013) www.theepochtimes.com/n3/326002-the-staggering-cost-of-economic-espionage-against-the-us/ (accessed 4 June 2018).
134 Ibid.

to combat the rising economic espionage threat, we should look for opportunities to apply existing legal frameworks or expand their scope through covering this new situation. International legal documents do not provide definition for economic and industrial espionage. Similarly, there is no specific framework to combat against cyberespionage; however, domestic legal systems describe espionage, industrial theft, and economic espionage as punishable crimes. Punishments envisaged for these crimes are applicable to those crimes, which are committed by cyber means. Additionally, at the international level, it is a gray area whether espionage is subject to certain limitations and punishments. However, by adding cyber and economic elements to espionage, this gray area becomes discrete, because huge amounts of economic and material damage occur due to economic and industrial cyberespionage activities. In this regard, along with the domestic regulations, states are looking for possible responses allowed under international law.

Due to the nature of information technologies and cyberespionage operations, they are inclined to be extraterritorial. For example, in many cases, states or corporations keep their data in cloud systems which most of the time are actually placed physically in a third country. Therefore, an attacker state is targeting not only the owner of the data but also a third country which is physically hosting the data of concern. In such cases, attributing the attack to a certain state and establishing the legal and factual link between the attack and the suspected states becomes challenging. In this regard, attribution methods and techniques should be studied and research conducted. This is outwith the scope of this study, however.

The next chapter will focus on the theoretical basis of cyberespionage activities and discuss several domestic and international legal responses to economic and industrial cyberespionage activities.

Cyberespionage under international legal theory

Why are states eager to enhance their cyberespionage capacity? What is the rationale behind their decision to apply such operations? The rational choice and game theory to international law offers comprehensive results in order to explain the rationale behind economic cyberespionage activities. It is crystal clear that states may decide to conduct cyberespionage activities as a result of cost-benefit analysis. The benefits, which are gained and expected to be gained, are greater than the cost and externalities of conducting cyberespionage.

Previous researchers have proven that weaker parties have been eager to challenge stronger ones and those weaker parties have been inclined to win the conflicts.[135] The underlying reason for such an outcome is the strategy adopted by the parties. While the stronger side focuses on and designs its strategy on attacking, the weaker side adopts direct defense and guerrilla warfare strategies, which paves the way for victory.[136] In the case of cyberespionage, infiltration, and attack activities, the above strategies of the parties reversed. The weaker party adopts a simultaneous direct attacking and guerrilla warfare strategy, while the stronger party, in order to protect its valuable assets, adopts a direct defense strategy. It is generally a better strategy to focus one's efforts on cyber offense, rather than defense.[137] The weaker party in this regard is a small group of experts conducting operations and infiltration activities against the stronger parties, which are well-protected servers and networks of state entities and companies. Therefore, actors have adopted certain protective measures called "active cyber defense" which enable the targeted actors to identify, target, and counterattack. In addition, the weaker party is likely to take advantage of the stronger party's dependence on cyberspace for four significant reasons.[138] First, the costs of cyber operations are low in comparison with traditional espionage or military activities. Second, determining the origin of cyber operations and attributing them to the weaker party is difficult. Therefore, the strong party would be hindered in responding conventionally to such an attack. Third, cyber attacks can confuse the enemy. Fourth, there is an underdeveloped legal framework to guide responses. Those four significant reasons provide an asymmetric advantage for the weaker side and may reduce conventional military dominance and superiority of the stronger party.

In some respects, there is an equilibrium on deciding and conducting cyberespionage activities. States can conduct or refrain from conducting cyberespionage activities under certain circumstances. Such a decision is subject to internal and external variables. The capabilities of states, effective use and allocation of resources and legal restrictions, on the one hand, and the capabilities of the target, the benefits to be gained

---

135 Ivan Arreguín-Toft, *How the Weak Win Wars, A Theory of Asymmetric Conflict*, Cambridge: Cambridge University Press (2005); T. V. Paul, *Asymmetric Conflicts: War Initiation by Weaker Powers*, Cambridge: Cambridge University Press (1994).
136 Ibid., 39.
137 Pierluigi Paganini, "FireEye World War C report – nation-state driven cyber attacks," Security Affairs RSS (3 October 2013) http://securityaffairs.co/wordpress/18294/security/fireeye-nation-state-driven-cyber-attacks.html (4 June 2018).
138 US-China Economic and Security Review Commission, Report to Congress (2008), 9 www.uscc.gov/sites/default/files/annual_reports/2008-Report-to-Congress-_0.pdf (accessed 4 June 2018).

Table 1.4 Strategies of stronger and weaker parties

Stronger party	Weaker party
Direct Defense	Direct Attack
Active Defense	Guerrilla Warfare

from the activity, international relations between states, and legal consequences of the actions affect the targeting process, on the other. Furthermore, the scenarios below illustrate the possible equilibrium while deciding to deploy cyberespionage activities.

First, a state might not want to perpetrate cyberespionage because it can use its capacity for more beneficial purposes, for example, by attacking another target. This is also related to the strategic allocation of resources. Either through cost-benefit analysis or through allocation of resources strategically, states can refrain from attacking a specific target. This equation is called coincidence of interest. "In this situation states are acting independently to achieve their best outcomes regardless of the behaviors of other states."[139] To illustrate whether sponsored by state or not, hacker groups are attacking other states' critical infrastructure and targeting only strategic sectors to collect, infiltrate and gain economic advantage; they are motivated to gain access and try to achieve their best outcome without pay attention to reactions of other states. In this sense, they are oblivious to any possible reaction or behavior of a targeted state and they are only motivated to gain an advantage of any kind without considering the reaction.

Second, many states receive no benefit from perpetrating cyberespionage and the few states that would benefit from cyberespionage are deterred from doing so by powerful states that want to prevent being attacked. In other words, many states refrain from attacking non-strategic targets due to inefficiency, or strategic targets due to being targeted by a strong opponent. This inactivity derives from the concept of coercion: such as cyber, diplomatic, economic, and military. In this regard, detecting pressure points and adopting appropriate measures hinder other states' capabilities to perform those activities.

Third, where two states decline to attack each other's systems in a bilateral repeated prisoner's dilemma, all the other states then decline to do so because of the coincidences of interest of coercion. Alternatively,

139 Jack L. Goldsmith and Eric Posner, *Limit of International Law*, Oxford: Oxford University Press (2005), 35.

it may be that the other states also face each other in bilateral prisoner dilemmas and therefore refrain from attacking because they fear retaliation from their (single) opponent.

As underlined by Deeks, "clear and objective surveillance norms that restrict current foreign surveillance practices can improve interstate relationships."[140] Therefore, legal norms and principles regulating and restricting surveillance and cyber infiltration activities will eventually contribute to interstate relations. Similarly, Baker states: "mutual trust between treaty parties increases when espionage affirms that the assurances provided are accurate. States will be more willing to cooperate with other states in the future if their espionage confirms that the assurances provided by these parties are truthful."[141] Contrary to Baker and Deeks, Buchan writes: "espionage represents a threat to the maintenance of international peace and security."[142]

Concluding remarks

While espionage operations have radically changed in terms of targets, purposes, actors, methods and means, we have discovered that traditional espionage activities have evolved into cyberespionage. Keeping in the mind the cyber operations conducted by states, there are no international norms or principles that explicitly or implicitly prohibit the usage of cyberespionage. As for the creation of customary norms in terms of cyberespionage or cyber attacks, we may recall how they occur. First, the actions of states turn into recurrent practices, and then the customary international norm is constituted by adding legal awareness to these behavioral patterns.[143] Likewise, an analogy can be established between cyberespionage and reconnaissance flights. States become irritated if targeted for cyberespionage, however, they are not currently inclined to pass rules and principles regulating cyberespionage.

The most effective solutions that will be implemented in the future are international cooperation and treaties.[144] There is a strong inclination

140 Ashley Deeks, "An international legal framework for surveillance," *Virginia Journal of International Law*, 55(2) (2015), 325.
141 Christopher D. Baker, "Tolerance of international espionage: A functional approach," *American University International Law Review*, 19(5) (2011), 1105.
142 Russel Buchan, "Cyber espionage and international law," in Nicholas Tsagourias and Russell Buchan (eds.), *Research Handbook on International Law and Cyberspace*, Cheltenham: Edward Elgar Publishing (2015), 177.
143 Öktem, *Uluslararası Teamül*, 521.
144 John Arquilla, "Cyberwar is already upon us," *Foreign Policy*, 27 February 2012 www.foreignpolicy.com/articles/2012/02/27/cyberwar_is_already_upon_us (accessed 4 June 2018).

to produce such legal documents, not at the international level yet, but at least bilaterally. In September 2015, President Barack Obama hosted President Xi Jinping of China on a state visit. Building on the two Memoranda of Understanding on Confidence Building Measures signed by the United States and China in November 2014, the two heads of state agreed not to conduct cyberespionage activities.[145] Then, in June 2017, China and Canada agreed not to conduct state-sponsored cyberespionage operations targeting trade secrets or other confidential business information.[146]

We have outlined several incidents and operations in this chapter that would constitute a legal base for state practice in the creation of customary international law. However, the recurrent practice of states practice is not solely sufficient for the creation customary international norm, there has to be *opinio juris* and state practice. The agreements covered above can be evaluated as *opinio juris* but only for the parties.[147] In the next chapter under domestic regulations we aim to discuss how such regulations may constitute *opinio juris* towards the creation of a customary international law for restricting cyberespionage operations. It is still a little early to assert, but such domestic regulations will eventually pave the way for the codification or creation of customary international law.

In the next chapter will discuss first the international responses to cyberespionage operations conducted by organs or agencies of states. Second, international responses to cyberespionage operations conducted by non-state actors (private actors) will be looked at in more detail. To conclude, comparative law responses to both will be examined

---

145 White House, "President Xi Jinping's State Visit to the United States" (25 September 2015) https://obamawhitehouse.archives.gov/the-press-office/2015/09/25/fact-sheet-president-xi-jinpings-state-visit-united-states (accessed 19 December 2017); "The United States and China agree that neither country's government will conduct or knowingly support cyber-enabled theft of intellectual property, including trade secrets or other confidential business information, with the intent of providing competitive advantages to companies or commercial sectors."

146 Joint Communiqué – 2nd Canada-China High-Level National Security and Rule of Law Dialogue, 22 June 2017 https://pm.gc.ca/eng/news/2017/06/22/joint-communique-2nd-canada-china-high-level-national-security-and-rule-law-dialogue (accessed 20 December 2017).

147 Michael N. Schmitt (ed.), *Tallinn Manual 2.0 on the International Law Applicable to Cyber Operations*, Cambridge: Cambridge University Press (2017), 169. The International Group of Experts who have drafted the Tallinn Manual 2.0 agreed that "customary international law does not prohibit espionage per se. However, they argued that cyberespionage has become so pervasive and detrimental that a new customary international law norm prohibiting it has crystallized, the Experts concurred that insufficient State practice and opinion juris on the matter exist to so conclude."

through Turkish, US and European approaches, which are all criminalizing cyberespionage activities. Such domestic and regional regulations can be considered a substantial indicator of *opinio juris*. The focus of the next chapter is on the regulations that seek to address wrongful acquisition and misappropriation of the data.

2 Legal responses to economic and industrial cyberespionage

Widespread employment of espionage in recent decades gives rise to fears the traditional methods of conducting international affairs and defending territory are inadequate.[1]

In the light of the explanations presented in the first chapter, it is acknowledged that cyberespionage activities, motivated by acquiring commercial and industrial assets, not only pose significant threats to economic and financial systems, but also governmental networks. Therefore, well-grounded counter mechanisms can be triggered in accordance with the profile of the attacker which is a state entity or agency or a private entity backed by a state or just a private entity.

First of all, if a state has been targeted by another state or a private entity backed by a state, then the targeted state may adopt certain measures in accordance with international law such as: declaring such activities as internationally wrongful acts and deploy countermeasures; seek treaty law responses accordingly such as terminating bilateral treaties due to fraudulence. In the case of state responsibility, we should inspect international legal documents restricting such activities or state practices according to appropriate legal responses and international forums to tackle economic cyberespionage. Although there are limited restrictions imposed on espionage activities by international norms, there are still several legal bases for targeted states to assert illegality of economic cyberespionage and to adopt legal arguments, under the domestic and international law.

Second, if a state has been targeted by a private entity and the host state is unaware of the situation then the targeted state may apply

1 Wesley L. Gould and Michael Barkun, *International Law and the Social Sciences*, Princeton: Princeton University Press (1970), 255.

international forums such as the WTO or trigger article 39 of the TRIPS Agreement or seek bilateral solutions to find and prosecute the suspects.

Third, in any case, states are eager to elevate their standards, domestic regulations, and civil-criminal remedies by criminalizing unauthorized access to computer systems, trade secret misappropriation, etc. The Tallinn Manual underlined that a state may exercise its jurisdiction: 1) over persons engaged in cyber activities on its territory; 2) over cyber infrastructure on its territory; and 3) extraterritorially, in accordance with international law.[2] In this regard, states criminalize certain activities depending on the outcome of cyberespionage. Many states do not have specific regulations dedicated to tackling cyberespionage, so the traditional legal approach offers to apply intellectual property crimes for such activities. In other words, a traditional legal approach takes into consideration the target of those activities and suggests a punishment accordingly. Therefore, regulations relating to cyber crimes and the protection of trade secrets are domestic legal tools if any private network is targeted by cyberespionage. There are also specific regulations to penalize economic and industrial espionage. Those regulations exist only under the American legal system, so we will analyze these regulations as well.

In order to give viable responses to cyberespionage activities legally, we should inspect legal documents for definitions, criminalized activities, and appropriate punishments for individuals and legal entities.

Legal responses to state cyberespionage

Cyberespionage during wartime

In addition to the explanations made under the section "Legality of wartime espionage," the legality of cyberespionage during wartime will be analyzed in this section. According to the Manual on International Law Applicable to Air and Missile Warfare, Rule 119, "acts of espionage are not prohibited under the law of international armed conflict."[3]

It is an accepted rule that "cyberespionage and other forms of information gathering directed at an adversary during an armed conflict does not violate the law of armed conflict."[4] The Tallinn Manual stated: "cyber espionage and other forms of information gathering

---

2 Schmitt, *Tallinn Manual*, 27.
3 HPCR, Manual on International Law; US Commander's Handbook on the Law of Naval Operations, COMDTPUB P5800.7A (2007) para. 12.9.
4 Schmitt, *Tallinn Manual*, 158.

directed at an adversary during an armed conflict does not violate the law of armed conflict. A member of the armed forces who has engaged in cyber espionage in enemy controlled territory loses the right to be a prisoner of war and may be treated as a spy if captured before rejoining the armed forces to which he or she belongs."[5] The International Group of Experts explicitly states that topics such as "cyber espionage, theft of intellectual property and a wide variety of criminal activities" are not addressed in the Tallinn Manual due to "application of the international law on uses of force and armed conflict plays little or no role."[6] Likewise, the International Group of Experts underlined the fact that "The development of further State practice notwithstanding, network intrusions, the deletion or destruction of data (even on a large scale) computer network exploitation, and data theft do not amount to a non-international armed conflict. The blocking of certain Internet functions and services would not, for example, suffice to trigger a noninternational armed conflict, nor would defacing governmental or other official websites."[7]

Nevertheless, the International Group of Experts agreed that cyberespionage operations could only target the information relating to a party of the conflict. "It is not cyberespionage for the purpose of this rule for a corporation located in the territory of a part to the conflict to use cyber means to surreptitiously gather information about the commercial activities of a corporation in the territory of another party to the conflict."[8] In other words, this rule does not cover activities out of scope of the conflict in question.

Cyberespionage during peacetime

As explained in the previous chapter, espionage activities during peacetime constitute a violation of several principles of international law. This rationale is also accepted in the case of peacetime cyberespionage activities. A state targeted by cyber operations, which are attributable to another state and constitute an internationally wrongful act, but do not amount to an armed attack, may respond with acts of retorsion or non-forcible countermeasures.

Keep in mind the explanations made by the Canadian Federal Court in 2007, "binding customary principles of ... international law prohibit interference with the sovereignty and domestic affairs of other states."[9]

5 Ibid.
6 Ibid., 18.
7 Ibid., 87–88.
8 Ibid.
9 Canadian Federal Court, Canadian Security Intelligence Service Act.

An equivalent attitude is embedded by the Tallinn Manual, under article 4, which states that "any interference by a state with cyber infrastructure aboard a platform, wherever located, that enjoys sovereign immunity constitutes a violation of sovereignty."[10]

As stated under article 6 of the Tallinn Manual, "a state bears international legal responsibility for a cyber operation attributable to it and which constitute a breach of an international obligation."[11] Likewise, according to article 9 of the Tallinn Manual, "a state injured by an internationally wrongful act may resort to proportionate countermeasures, including cyber countermeasures, against the responsible State."[12]

The International Group of Experts, who drafted the Tallinn Manual 2.0, accepted that "if an aspect of a cyberespionage operation is unlawful under international law, it renders the cyberespionage unlawful."[13]

The principle of sovereignty, the prohibition of use of force or intervention or threat of use of force can be violated by cyberespionage operations. Those principles of international law constitute a legal basis for invoking the breach of an international obligation and the Responsibility of States for Internationally Wrongful Acts due to being targeted by cyberespionage activities.

Prohibition on use of force

Pursuant to article 2(4) of the UN Charter, "all members shall refrain in their international relations from the threat or use of force against the territorial integrity or political independence of any state, or in any other manner inconsistent with the Purposes of the United Nations." This prohibition is prescribed to achieve the purpose of the United Nations as it is stipulated under the first article: "to maintain international peace and security." The UN Charter did not provide any criteria to define such kinds of acts that amount to the use of force. The scale and effects test, argued in the Nicaragua Case of ICJ, is accepted to be an appropriate tool for determining whether an act amounts to an armed attack or not.[14]

Regarding whether cyberespionage or cyber attacks can constitute an armed attack, there are two different views. The first view accepts that

---

10 Schmitt, *Tallinn Manual*, 23.
11 Ibid., 29.
12 Ibid., 36.
13 Schmitt, *Tallinn Manual 2.0*, 170. Rule 32 of the Manual states that "Although peacetime cyberespionage by states does not per se violate international law, the method by which it is carried out might do so."
14 ICJ, Military and Paramilitary Activities in and Against Nicaragua, para. 195.

cyber operations cannot amount to an armed attack since article 2(4) of the UN Charter has been interpreted restrictively to only prohibit conduct that produces human casualties and destruction of property.[15] Although the ordinary meaning of "force" is clearly broad enough to include both armed and unarmed forms of coercion, use of force is traditionally understood as "to imply a military attack an armed attack by the organized military, naval or air forces of a state."[16] However, cyber operations do not cause any human casualties or physical harm. Secondly, the *travaux préparatoires* of the UN Charter indicates that the prohibition of use of force was not intended to include economic coercion and political pressure.[17] Additionally, article 41 of the UN Charter refers to "interruption of ... communication" as a "measure not involving armed force," thus, certain types of cyber operations cannot be assessed under the prohibition of article 2/4. In light of above reasons, cyber operations cannot be regarded as use of force.

On the contrary, the second view accepts that "cyber operations fall under the prohibition of article 2(4) of the UN Charter once *their effects* are comparable to those likely to result from kinetic, chemical, biological or nuclear weaponry."[18] This approach has also been accepted by International Group of Experts under the Tallinn Manual: "a cyber operation constitutes a use of force when its scale and effects are comparable to non-cyber operations rising to the level of a use of force."[19] This view is supported by two arguments. First, article 2(4) states only "threat or use of force," but does not specifically mention what kind of threat or force.[20] As highlighted by the International Court of Justice, in its Advisory Opinion on the Legality of the Threat or Use of Nuclear

15 Dinstein, *War, Agression and Self Defence*, 208: "an armed attack presupposes a use of force producing (or liable to produce) serious consequences, epitomized by territorial intrusions, human casualties or considerable destruction of property."
16 Ian Brownlie, *International Law and the Use of Force by States*, Oxford: Clarendon (1963), 362.
17 A Brazilian proposal to extend the prohibition to "the threat or use of economic measures in any manner inconsistent with the purposes of the United Nations" was rejected at the San Francisco Conference: Documents of the United Nations Conference on International Organization, Vol. VI, 1945, 559, 720–21.
18 Ibid. Dinstein, *War, Agression and Self Defence*, 80.
19 Schmitt, *Tallinn Manual*, 47.
20 Albert Randelzhofer, "Use of Force" in Rudolf Bernhardt (ed.), *Encyclopedia of Public International Law*, Vol. 4, Amsterdam: North Holland Publishing (1982), 268: "Corresponding to the prevailing and correct view, force in Art. 2/4 is limited to armed forces. It must be admitted that the wording of Art. 2(4) of the Charter alone gives no clear answer to this dispute. But para. 7 of the preamble of the Charter states one of the aims of the United Nations to be 'that armed force shall not be used, save in the common interest', and Art. 44 supports the view that the Charter also uses the

Weapons,[21] "article 51 does not refer to specific weapons: it applies to any armed attack, regardless of the weapon employed,[22] it does not matter what specific means kinetic or electronic are used to bring it about, but the end result must be that violence occurs or is threatened."[23]

In addition to that, Brownlie asked whether use of weapons such as bacteriological, biological and chemical devices, which do not involve any explosive effect, can be amount to use of force?[24] Although academics garnered at that time that they should be employed with weapons that are more orthodox to be qualified as use of force, Brownlie argued that the "use of such weapons could be assimilated to the use of force as they are employed for the destruction of life and property."[25] Likewise, Dinniss argues that in order to apply the prohibition of use of force in the Charter, the unique characteristic of computer network attacks should be taken into account, as ICJ adopted the same approach in its Nuclear Weapons advisory opinion.[26] For example, Stuxnet is a tailored cyber weapon designed to target specific SCADA systems, so malfunctioning of the system causes physical destruction of the equipment. Therefore, "the use of cyber operations as an offensive or defensive tool designed to cause death or injury to persons or the destruction of objects and infrastructure, irrespective of whether such destruction involves physical damage, functional harm, or a combination of both,"[27] can be accepted as use of force.

Second, if a cyber attack can create "severe damage to property or even human fatalities (as a result, e.g., of the shutdown of computers controlling waterworks and dams, leading to the flooding of inhabited areas), it would qualify as an armed attack."[28] Therefore, certain legal

notion of force in cases where it apparently means armed force. The prevailing view is further supported by the teleological interpretation of Art. 2(4)."
21 ICJ, Advisory Opinion on Legality of the Threat or Use of Nuclear Weapons (1996) ICJ Reports 226, 254.
22 See Yoram Dinstein, "Computer network attacks and self-defense," *International Law Studies*, 76 (1999), 103.
23 Dinstein, *War, Agression and Self Defence*, 88.
24 Brownlie, *International Law*, 362.
25 Ibid.
26 Dinniss, *Cyber Warfare and the Laws of War*, 65.
27 Nils Melzer, *Cyberwarfare and International Law*, Geneva: UNIDIR (2011), 7: "Conspicuous examples of a use of 'force' within the meaning of article 2(4) of the UN Charter, therefore, would be cyber operations manipulating target computers systems so as to cause a meltdown in a nuclear power station, or opening the floodgates of a dam above a densely populated area, or disabling a busy airport's air traffic control during bad weather conditions, each with potentially horrendous consequences in terms of death, injury and destruction." http://unidir.org/files/publications/pdfs/cyberwarfare-and-international-law-382.pdf (accessed 4 June 2018).
28 Dinstein, *War, Aggression and Self Defence*, 212.

scholars argued that if a cyber attack does not cause harm to persons or physical damage to property, but creates catastrophic, severe effects,[29] or extremely adverse effects,[30] such an attack should be qualified as an armed attack. Likewise, according to Melnitzky, "prior to the Internet, looting on such a scale could only have been accomplished by a military occupation. The effects-based approach requires that a cyber attack must cause damage only previous possible by traditional military force is therefore satisfied."[31] In this sense, cyberespionage, which violates the confidentiality and integrity of a network as a cyber attack, but also violates commercial secrets, can be categorized as use of force. In addition to that, it should be underlined that article 2/4 of the UN Charter prohibits the use of force "regardless of its gravity, magnitude, scale or duration."[32] ICJ noted this in the Nicaragua Case, by stating that even a minor act of interstate force is prohibited under the article 2/4 of the UN Charter.[33]

29 Schmitt, *Tallinn Manual*, 55–56: "The classical scenario illustrating the division of opinion (among experts on this issue) is a cyber incident directed against the New York Stock Exchange that causes the market to crash. Experts were divided over the characterization of such an event. Some of the experts were unprepared to label it as an armed attack because they were not satisfied that mere financial loss constitutes damages for this purpose. Others emphasized the catastrophic effects such a crash would occasion and therefore regards them as sufficient to characterize the cyber operation as an armed attack. By the same approach, a cyber operation directed against major components of a State's critical infrastructure that causes severe, albeit not destructive, effects would qualify as an armed attack."
30 Roscini, *Cyber Operations and the Use of Force*, 55.
31 Alexander Melnitzky, "Defending America Against Chinese cyber espionage through the use of active defenses," *Cardozo Journal of International Comparative Law*, 20 (2012), 566. For opposing views that cyberespionage cannot be qualified as use of force, because there is insufficient state practice see: Russell Buchan, "Cyberattacks: unlawful uses of force or prohibited interventions?" *Journal of Conflict and Security Law*, 17 (2012), 211. Russel Buchan, "Cyber espionage and international law," in Nicholas Tsagourias and Russell Buchan (eds.), *Research Handbook on International Law and Cyberspace*, Cheltenham: Edward Elgar Publishing (2015), 187; David Fidler, "Tinker, tailor, soldier, duqu: why cyber espionage is more dangerous than you think," *International Journal of Critical Infrastructures*, 5 (2012), 28–29: "no government regards cyber espionage of any kind as a prohibited use of force."
32 Brownlie, *International Law*, 214 and 432; Dinstein, *War, Aggression and Self-Defence*, 175; ICJ, Corfu Channel (*United Kingdom of Great Britain and Northern Ireland v. Albania*) (Merits), Separate Opinion by Judge Alvarez, 1949, 47. "The minesweeping operation undertaken by British ships in the Corfu Strait was in fact a violation of Albanian sovereignty. The Court must reaffirm, as often as the occasion arises, that intervention and all kinds of forcible action are not permissible, in any form or on any pretext in relations between States."
33 ICJ, Military and Paramilitary Activities in and against Nicaragua, para. 195: "sending by or on behalf of a State of armed bands, groups, irregulars or mercenaries, which

It should also be noted that the militarization of cyberspace is a well-known fact.[34] Due to strategic or military concerns, many states have, or want to acquire, offensive cyber weapons, have set up cyber commands within their military organization and adopt cyber warfare programs or manuals.[35] In this regard, in the presence of such practices of states, indicate that cyber operations can be considered as use of force. Many scholars support and side with the second view which is the recognition of cyber operations as a form of use of force, as Dinstein states:

> from a legal perspective, there is no reason to differentiate between kinetic and electronic means of attack. A premeditated destructive CNA can qualify as an armed attack just as much as a kinetic attack bringing about the same – or similar – results. The crux of the matter is not the medium at hand (a computer server in lieu of, say, an artillery battery), but the violent consequences of the action taken. If there is a cause and effect chain between the CNA and these violent consequences, it is immaterial that they were produced by high rather than low technology.[36]

Cyber operations need not amount to use of force within the meaning of article 2/4 of the UN Charter to be internationally wrongful. Such

carry out acts of armed force against another State of such gravity as to amount to (inter alia) an actual armed attack conducted by regular forces, or its substantial involvement therein. Court does not believe that the concept of 'armed attack' includes not only acts by armed bands where such acts occur on a significant scale but also assistance to rebels in the form of the provision of weapons or logistical or other support. Such assistance may be regarded as a threat or use of force, or amount to intervention in the internal or external affairs of other states. It is also clear that it is the state which is the victim of an armed attack which must form and declare the view that it has been so attacked."

34 Myriam Dunn Cavelty, *The Militarization of Cyberspace: Why Less May Be Better*, NATO CCD COE Publications (2012); Myriam Dunn Cavelty, *The Militarisation of Cyber Security as a Source of Global Tension, Strategic Trends Analysis*, Zurich, ETH: Center for Security Studies (2012). Kristin Bergtora Sandvik, *Towards a Militarization of Cyberspace? Cyberwar as an Issue of International Law*, Oslo: PRIO Papers (2012); Jens Ringsmose and Karsten Friis (eds.), *Conflict in Cyber Space Theoretical, Strategic and Legal Perspectives*, New York: Routledge (2016).

35 Countries which currently have cyber command: United States, United Kingdom, South Korea, China, NATO based in Tallinn, Germany, India, Iran, Russia, Israel, Netherlands, France, Turkey. Jennifer Valentino-Devries and Danny Yadron, "Cataloging the world's cyberforces," *Wall Street Journal* (11 October 2015): the journal's research shows that 29 countries now have formal military or intelligence units dedicated to offensive cyberefforts; 49 countries have bought off-the-shelf hacking software; 63 countries use cybertools for surveillance, either domestically or internationally.

36 Dinstein, "Computer network attacks and self-defense," 103.

operations can violate certain obligations and principles derived from customary international law and treaty law.

Internationally wrongful act

States are considered responsible for their internationally wrongful acts.[37] In 2001, the International Law Commission adopted draft articles on the responsibility of states for internationally wrongful acts. Although it is not a binding document, it set out the principles and norms on this topic. The very first articles defined the elements of internationally wrongful acts. There is an internationally wrongful act of a state when conduct consisting of an action or omission: 1) is attributable to the state under international law; and 2) constitutes a breach of an international obligation of the state.[38]

Moreover, cyberespionage activities can be legally categorized under internationally wrongful acts due to contradiction between well-established international law principles, territorial sovereign equality and non-intervention.[39] Illegality of the cyberespionage

37 CarrieLyn D. Guymon (ed.), *Digest of United States Practice in International Law*, US Department of State, Chapter 18 (2014), 738: www.state.gov/documents/organiza-tion/244504.pdf (accessed 4 June 2018): "A State is responsible for an internationally wrongful act when there is an act or omission that is attributable to it under international law that constitutes a breach of an international obligation of the State. Cyber activities may constitute internationally wrongful acts if they are inconsistent with a primary rule of international law and are attributed to a State under the secondary rules on State responsibility. A State is legally responsible for cyber activities undertaken through 'proxy actors' who act on the State's instructions or under its direction or control. If a State exercises a sufficient degree of control over a person or group of persons committing an internationally wrongful act, the State assumes responsibility for the act just as if the State had committed the act itself. These rules apply to conduct online just as they do offline, and they ensure that States cannot hide behind putatively private actors in engaging in internationally wrongful conduct."

38 UN International Law Commission, Draft articles on Responsibility of States for Internationally Wrongful Acts, with commentaries (A/56/10) *Yearbook of the International Law Commission*, 2(2) (2001), art. 2 http://legal.un.org/ilc/texts/instruments/english/commentaries/9_6_2001.pdf (accessed 4 June 2018).

39 Catherine Lotrionte, "Countering state-sponsored cyber economic espionage under international law," *North Carolina Journal of International Law*, 40 (2014), 496: "economic espionage, as a highly intrusive coercive act into the economic and political freedoms of a state, may constitute a wrongful act of intervention in violation of the customary norm." The use of countermeasures can provide states with a legal basis for effective responses to economic espionage, buying time for the potential establishment of international consensus to prohibit cyber methods of IP theft for competitive advantage through a new treaty, state practice or new interpretations of WTO agreements as applicable to economic espionage.

may result from violation of any obligation under international law. "Interstate computer network exploitation for the purposes of intelligence gathering, electronic dissemination of hostile propaganda, or denial of service attacks,"[40] can be considered as a violation of the sovereignty of the targeted state and the customary principle of nonintervention, even if they do not qualify as use of force within the meaning of article 2(4) of the UN Charter. Likewise, "non-destructive cyber operations intruding into computer-based archives, documents and correspondence of a foreign diplomatic mission, or interfering with the mission's free communication,"[41] is violating international obligations of the receiving state under Vienna Convention on Diplomatic Relations.[42]

Both the Permanent Court of International Justice (PCIJ) and the International Court of Justice (ICJ) applied the principles of the Responsibility of States for Internationally Wrongful Acts as those where "every internationally wrongful act of a State entails the international responsibility of that State."[43] For instance, in the *Phosphates in Morocco* case, the PCIJ underlined an internationally wrongful act against another state.[44] The *Corfu Channel* case is significant for cyberespionage because, as the ICJ stated: "nothing was attempted by the Albanian authorities to prevent the disaster. These grave omissions involve the international responsibility of Albania."[45] Attributing an omission and its legal consequences to a state is providing a viable analogy for cyberespionage operations, because most of the time states act reluctantly to take preventive measures against criminal networks responsible for cyber attacks.

In the *Rainbow Warrior* case, the arbitral tribunal concluded that "in the international law field there is no distinction between contractual and tortious responsibility, so that any violation by a State of any obligation, of whatever origin, gives rise to State responsibility and consequently, to the duty of reparation."[46] This interpretation also covers the general principles of international law such as territorial integrity and non-intervention. The interpretation of international wrongful acts by

40 Melzer, *Cyberwarfare and International Law*, 9.
41 Ibid.
42 Vienna Convention on Diplomatic Relations, arts 24, 27 and 45(a).
43 UN International Law Commission, supra fn. 38, see art. 1.
44 PCIJ, Phosphates in Morocco (Judgment) (1938), Series A/B, No. 74, 10 www.icj-cij.org/pcij/serie_AB/AB_74/01_Phosphates_du_Maroc_Arret.pdf (accessed 21 July 2015).
45 ICJ, Corfu Channel Case (*UK* v. *Albania*) (1949) para. 23.
46 ICJ, Rainbow Warrior (*New Zealand* v. *France*) (1990) 278 http://legal.un.org/riaa/cases/vol_XX/215–284.pdf (accessed 21 July 2015).

the ICJ was widened in later years. In the *Barcelona Traction* case, the ICJ noted that

> an essential distinction should be drawn between the obligations of a State towards the international community as a whole and *vis-à-vis* another State. By their very nature, the former is the concern of all states. In view of the importance of the rights involved, all States can be held to have a legal interest in their protection; they are obligations *erga omnes*.[47]

Apart from attribution problems, if a state engages in activities neither prohibited nor regulated by international law such as espionage, state responsibility can only be asserted if such activities violate other norms of international law, such as protection of diplomatic communication, good faith while concluding a treaty, etc. Thus, the legal base for asserting illegality of espionage should be linked to existing international law principles, norms and values, either *jus cogen* norms or *erga omnes* obligations.

The breach of international obligation has two distinctive legal consequences. First, "the State responsible for the internationally wrongful act is under an obligation: (1) to cease that act, if it is continuing; (2) to offer appropriate assurances and guarantees of non-repetition if circumstances so require."[48] Second, "the responsible State is under an obligation to make full reparation for the injury caused by the internationally wrongful act. Injury includes any damage, whether material or moral, caused by the internationally wrongful act of a State."[49] Furthermore, the responsible state is under obligation to "re-establish the situation which existed before the wrongful act was committed"[50] and the responsible state is under obligation to "compensate for the damage caused thereby, insofar as such damage is not made good by restitution."[51] Finally, if restitution or compensation becomes inadequate, the responsible state is under obligation to "give satisfaction for the injury."[52]

On the other hand, internationally wrongful acts create new rights on behalf of injured states. The injured or targeted states have the right

---

47 ICJ, The Barcelona Traction (*Belgium* v. *Spain*) (1970) 32 www.icj-cij.org/docket/files/50/5387.pdf (accessed 21 July 2015).
48 UN International Law Commission, supra fn. 38, see art. 30.
49 Ibid., art. 31.
50 Ibid., art. 35.
51 Ibid., art. 36.
52 Ibid., art. 37.

to invoke responsibility,[53] but limited rights to take countermeasures.[54] Article 46 is well-tailored especially for global mass surveillance or espionage activities conducted without any limitations: "where several States are injured by the same internationally wrongful act, each injured State may separately invoke the responsibility of the State which has committed the internationally wrongful act."[55]

This legal ground can be invoked by other states, which faced the same internationally wrongful act. For instance, in relation to mass surveillance communications' content and metadata, intelligence-gathering activity "amounts to a systematic interference with the right to respect for the privacy of communications, and requires a correspondingly compelling justification."[56] As stated in the Report of the Special Rapporteur on the promotion and protection of human rights and fundamental freedoms while countering terrorism, "bulk access technology is indiscriminately corrosive of online privacy and impinges on the very essence of the right guaranteed by the UN's International Covenant on Civil and Political Rights."[57]

To this end, article 49 of the draft articles of the Responsibility of States for Internationally Wrongful Acts stated, "an injured State may only take countermeasures against a State which is responsible for an internationally wrongful act in order to induce that State to comply with its obligations." In this regard, countermeasure and retorsion will be discussed in the next part.

COUNTERMEASURES AGAINST CYBERESPIONAGE

Considering industrial and economic cyberespionage activities as economic warfare,[58] cyber-based countermeasures or non-cyber-based

---

53 Ibid., arts 42–48.
54 Ibid., arts 49–53.
55 Ibid., art. 46.
56 UN Report of the Special Rapporteur on the promotion and protection of human rights and fundamental freedoms while countering terrorism (23 September 2014) A/69/397 para. 59 http://daccess-dds-ny.un.org/doc/UNDOC/GEN/N14/545/19/PDF/N1454519.pdf?OpenElement (accessed 15 July 2015).
57 Ibid., para. 59.
58 Karl Zemanek, "Economic warfare," in Rudolf Bernhardt, *Encyclopedia of Public International Law*, Vol. 3 Amsterdam: North Holland Publishing (1981), 158: "Generally speaking, the term economic warfare indicates a hostile relationship between two or more States in which at least one endeavors to damage the economy of the other(s) for economic, political or military ends. The term is further used to describe the sum of measures and countermeasures which the States involved take in this context."

countermeasures can be adopted against states that constitute internationally wrongful acts.[59]
Pursuant to article 51 of the draft articles of the Responsibility of States for Internationally Wrongful Acts, "countermeasures must be commensurate with the injury suffered, taking into account the gravity of the internationally wrongful act and the rights in question." Therefore, countermeasures must meet the requirements of necessity and proportionality, but must also be designed to induce the state to return to compliance with its international obligations. According to article 52, before taking countermeasures, an injured state shall: (a) call on the responsible state, to fulfill its obligations; (b) notify the responsible state of any decision to take countermeasures and offer to negotiate with that state. However, even before following the above procedure, the injured state may take such urgent countermeasures as are necessary to preserve its rights. With regard to article 53, countermeasures shall be terminated as soon as the responsible state has complied with its obligations.

The International Law Commission categorized countermeasures as sanctions, retorsion and reprisals. While retorsion is a lawful response to a wrongful act, reprisal is a reaction to an internationally wrongful act by the injured party against the offending state and generally involves the use of force.[60] Applying a cyber blockade or cyber containment in order to paralyze whole IT systems and related infrastructures can qualify as cyber base countermeasures.

RETORSION AGAINST CYBERESPIONAGE

As Shaw explained, "retorsion is the adoption by one state of an unfriendly and harmful act, which is nevertheless lawful, as a method of retaliation against the injurious legal activities of another state."[61] In other words, retorsion remains within the boundaries of law.[62] According to the ILC, any kind of action categorized as retorsion aims to deprive the responsible state of advantages from its offense.[63] To illustrate, retorsion can be breaking diplomatic relations, reducing economic

59 Guymon, *Digest of United States Practice In International Law*, 738.
60 Gaetano Arangio-Ruiz, *Third Report on State Responsibility*, A/CN.4/440 Yearbook of International Law Commission, Vol. II (1) (1991) para. 24–25 http://legal.un.org/ilc/documentation/english/a_cn4_440.pdf (accessed 4 June 2018).
61 Shaw, *International Law*, 1128.
62 Jan Klabbers, *International Law*, Cambridge: Cambridge University Press (2013), 168.
63 Arangio-Ruiz, *Third Report on State* Responsibility, para. 16–17.

support, imposing trade restrictions or visa requirements.[64] The ILC illustrated acts of retorsion as "limitations upon normal diplomatic relations, or other contacts, embargoes of various kinds or withdrawal of voluntary aid programs."[65] Schachter mentions that typical examples of retorsion include "rupture of diplomatic relations, cessation of trade in general or in specific areas, non-recognition of acts of the offending government, denial of benefits of available to the offending government, curtailment of migration from offending government."[66]

After the Snowden revelations, many countries passed new regulations or amended existing laws to oblige US technology firms to comply with provisions prohibiting data about their citizens from being transferred to other countries. According to Castro, "new regulations could cost U.S. IT services companies up to 35 billion dollars in revenue over the next three years."[67] To illustrate, Brazil initially declared that the Microsoft Outlook service would not be used anymore, and then a German company decided to use Deutsche Telekom rather than a US-based company for cloud computing services.[68]

64 Shaw, *International Law*, 1128: "…expulsion or restrictive control of aliens, as well as various economic and travel restriction."
65 Commentaries on the Draft Articles on Responsibility of States for Internationally Wrongful Acts, Yearbook of International Law Commission, Vol. II (2) (2001), 128.
66 Oscar Schachter, *International Law in Theory and Practice*, Leiden: Martinus Nijhoff Publishers (1991), 198. See also, Antonio Cassese, *International Law*, Oxford: Oxford University Press (2001), 244: according to Cassese, retorsion is "any retaliatory act by which a State responds, by an unfriendly act not amounting to a violation of international law, to either (a) a breach of international law or (b) an unfriendly act by another State." He gives examples of "the breaking off of diplomatic relations, discontinuance or reduction of trade/ investment, withholding economic assistance, expulsion of nationals, heavy fiscal duties on goods from the offending State, strict passport regulations."
67 Daniel Castro, "How much will PRISM cost the US cloud computing industry?," *Information Technology & Innovation Foundation* (August 2013) www2.itif.org/2013-cloud-computing-costs.pdf (accessed 4 June 2018); Michael Hickins, "Spying fears abroad hurt US tech firms," *Wall Street Journal*, 3 February 2014 online.wsj.com/news/articles/SB10001424052702303743604579350611848246016 or https://web.archive.org/web/20141215234339/http://www.wsj.com/news/articles/SB100014240527023037436 04579350611848246016 (accessed 4 June 2018) or wikileaks.org/hackingteam/emails/emailid/310058 (accessed 4 June 2018); Elizabeth Dwoskin, "New report: Snowden revelations hurt US companies," Wall Street Journal Digits Blog (30 July 2014) http://blogs.wsj.com/digits/2014/07/30/new-report-snowden-revelations-hurt-u-s-companies/ (accessed 4 June 2018).
68 Claire Cain Miller, "Revelations of NSA spying cost US tech companies," *New York Times* (21 March 2014) www.nytimes.com/2014/03/22/business/fallout-from-snowden-hurting-bottom-lineof-tech-companies.html (accessed 4 June 2018).

LEGAL RATIONALE

The fundamental question with regard to internationally wrongful acts and economic cyberespionage and setting up the legal rationale between them, is whether economic espionage is sufficient and effective for invoking the principles of states' responsibility. The basic legal argument to invoke state responsibility with regard to economic cyberespionage is state sovereignty, which also covers the very concept of economic sovereignty. Whether the operation targets public or private infrastructure, states enjoy sovereignty on both of them. According to Schmitt, a target state can invoke the principle of sovereignty if only "the cyber operation destroys or alters data or somehow makes the cyber infrastructure operate in a manner in which it is not intended to operate."[69] In other words, if physical damage or injury occurs, then the targeted state can invoke the principle of sovereignty against the targeting state. However, cyberespionage activities, even if such activities were conducted only for monitoring networks, can cause damage to the targeted state.

A targeted state should implement additional protection mechanisms because all of the existing cyber defense structures have been breached. For instance, after data breaches, *Petrobras* initiated a new data protection program costing "3.9 billion Brazilian Real (approximately 900 million US Dollars) in security with 3000 employees engaged in the area."[70] Additionally, according to the report published by the Center for Strategic and International Studies, it is estimated that cyber crime and economic espionage cost 445 billion USD annually to the world economy.[71] Further, economic costs and effects of a breach occur sometimes in the long run: for instance, the F-35 Lightning II Joint Strike Fighter program was seriously damaged and costs increased

---

69 Michael N. Schmitt, "Cyber responses 'by the numbers' in international law," *EJIL* (2015) www.ejiltalk.org/cyber-responses-by-the-numbers-in-international-law/ (accessed 15 July 2015); (according to Findler, economic espionage does not constitute internationally wrongful acts at all to trigger state responsibility. See, David P. Fidler, "Economic cyber espionage and international law: controversies involving government acquisition of trade secrets through cyber technologies," *ASIL*, 17(10) (2013) www.asil.org/insights/volume/17/issue/10/economic-cyber-espionage-and-international-law-controversies-involving (accessed 15 July 2015).

70 Joe Leahy, "Brazil's Petrobras to invest heavily in data security," *Financial Times* (18 September 2013) www.ft.com/cms/s/0/f3195d0a-2081-11e3-9a9a-00144feab7de.html#axzz3hzSQnxdS (accessed 15 July 2015).

71 McAfee, "Net losses: estimating the global cost of cybercrime" (June 2014) www.mcafee.com/us/resources/reports/rp-economic-impact-cybercrime2.pdf (accessed 15 July 2015).

steadily over time due to alleged Chinese economic cyberespionage operations.[72]

To this end, economic cyberespionage operations actually create damage to the targeted state and provide enough legal basis for asserting a violation of state sovereignty, which triggers state responsibility under internationally wrongful acts. Economic cyberespionage operations might violate treaty law obligations, which allow the targeted state to invoke legal mechanisms under treaty law.

International treaty law and cyberespionage

In 2013, Timor-Leste lodged a complaint against Australia and claimed that it was conducting espionage during the negotiations of a treaty between Australia and the Democratic Republic of Timor-Leste on Certain Maritime Arrangements in the Timor Sea (CMATS) in 2004.[73] Timor-Leste argued that Australia bugged cabinet offices of the Timor-Leste government during the negotiations for a petroleum and gas treaty in 2004, so the treaty should be declared void or invalid. However, shortly after the declaration of independence of Timor-Leste, the government of Australia declared that, "it recognizes as compulsory ipso facto and without specific agreement, in relation to any other State accepting the same obligation, the jurisdiction of the International Court of Justice in conformity with paragraph 2 of article 36 of the Statute of the Court."[74] In this context, Timor-Leste could not initiate a case before the ICJ, but Timor-Leste instituted arbitral proceedings at the Permanent Court of Arbitration[75] in accordance with the Timor Sea Treaty.[76]

---

72 David Alexander, "Theft of F-35 design data is helping U.S. adversaries – Pentagon," Reuters (19 June 2013) www.reuters.com/article/2013/06/19/usa-fighter-hacking-idUSL2N0EV0T320130619 (accessed 15 July 2015); Pierluigi Paganini, "Snowden reveals that China stole plans for a new F-35 aircraft fighter" *Security Affairs* (19 January 2015) http://securityaffairs.co/wordpress/32437/intelligence/china-stole-plans-f-35-aircraft.html (accessed 15 July 2015); "Plans of F-35," *Der Spiegel* www.spiegel.de/media/media-35687.pdf (accessed 15 July 2015).

73 Treaty between Australia and The Democratic Republic of Timor-Leste on Certain Maritime Arrangements in the Timor Sea (adopted 12 January 2006, entry into force, 23 February 2007) ATS 12; Australian Minister for Foreign Affairs, "Arbitration under the Timor Sea Treaty" (3 May 2013) http://foreignminister.gov.au/releases/2013/bc_mr_130503.html (accessed 4 June 2018).

74 Statute of the International Court of Justice www.icj-cij.org/jurisdiction/?p1=5&p2=1&p3=3&code=AU (accessed 21 June 2015).

75 PCA, *Timor-Leste v. Australia*, 2013–16 (2013).

76 Timor Sea Treaty between the Government of East Timor and the Government of Australia, ATS 13 (adopted 20 May 2002 entered into force 2 April 2003).

In 2010, it was revealed that the NSA granted the legal authority to intercept communications of 193 governments, intergovernmental organizations and other entities for foreign intelligence purposes, including Timor-Leste.[77] Likewise, in 2013, the Australian Security Intelligence Organization (ASIO) seized electronic and paper files from the office of the lawyer representing East Timor in the arbitration tribunal and a key witness in the Timor case, a former spy turned whistle-blower, has been arrested in a separate raid.[78]

Timor-Leste's Canberra-based legal advisor, Bernard Collaery stated that:

> the documents reveal that the Director General of the Australian Secret Intelligence Service and his deputy instructed a team of ASIS (Australian Secret Intelligence Service) technicians to travel to East Timor in an elaborate plan using Australian aid programs relating to the renovation and construction of the cabinet offices in Dili, East Timor, to insert listening devices into walls to be constructed under an Australian aid program.[79]

On 12 December 2013, Timor-Leste lodged an application before the ICJ and requested the ICJ declare "the seizure by Australia of the documents and data violated (1) the sovereignty of Timor-Leste and (2) its property and other rights under international law and that Australia must immediately return the documents and data."[80]

A year later, the ICJ declared by 12 votes to four, "Australia shall ensure that the content of the seized material is not in any way or at any time used by any person or persons to the disadvantage of Timor-Leste

---

77 NSA, In the Matter of Foreign Governments, Foreign Factions, Foreign Entities and Foreign-Based Political Organizations, 16 July 2010 https://search.edwardsnowden.com/docs/ExhibitF20140630 (accessed 21 July 2015).

78 Mark Colvin, "Lawyer representing E. Timor alleges ASIO agents raided his practice," ABC (3 December 2013); Katharine Murphy and Lenore Taylor, "Timor-Leste spy case: 'witness held, and lawyer's office raided by ASIO,'" *Guardian* (3 December 2013) www.theguardian.com/world/2013/dec/03/timor-leste-spy-witness-held-lawyers-office-raided-asio (accessed 21 July 2015). The senior retired Australian Secret Intelligence Service (ASIS) agent, who is a prime witness in the Timorese espionage case against Australia in the international courts, was detained and searched. The whistleblower intended to provide "credible direct evidence" of the bugging of the Timorese cabinet rooms in 2004.

79 Ibid.

80 ICJ (*Timor-Leste* v. *Australia*) (Application) (2013) 5, 6 www.icj-cij.org/docket/files/156/17962.pdf (accessed 21 June 2015).

until the present case has been concluded."[81] Furthermore, the ICJ stated, "Australia shall not interfere in any way in communications between Timor-Leste and its legal advisers."[82]

According to this subject, this is the first case which includes cyberespionage, economic espionage and application of international treaty law provisions. Thus, Timor-Leste has several legal grounds not only by to asserting the CMATS treaty is void or invalid, but also illegality of cyberespionage or economic espionage conducted by Australia that aimed to gain an advanced position in negotiations of the oil and petroleum treaty.

Although there is not any specific reference to cyberespionage or cyber attacks under the Vienna Convention, we consider that existing principles under the Convention can be violated due to such operations.

VIOLATION OF GOOD FAITH PRINCIPLE

Governing international law principles on treaties, whether bilateral or multilateral, are enshrined under the Vienna Convention on the Law of Treaties (VCLT or the Convention) which concluded in Vienna on 23 May 1969. The Convention set the principles to determine what a treaty is, how to conclude, terminate, amend and so on. The scope of the Convention was only about the treaties between states, not with other international subjects of international law.[83] According to the Convention:

> Treaty means an international agreement concluded between States in written form and governed by international law, whether embodied in a single instrument or in two or more related instruments and whatever its particular designation.

This definition indicates several elements for documents to become a treaty. First, a treaty has to be international. Second, treaties should be concluded between states, which excludes treaties between states and other subjects of international law. The ICJ in the *Anglo-Iranian*

81 ICJ, (*Timor-Leste* v. *Australia*) (Judgment) (2013) 8 www.icj-cij.org/docket/files/156/18090.pdf (accessed 21 June 2015).

82 Daniel Hurst, "Australia has violated Timor-Leste's sovereignty, UN court told," *Guardian* (20 January 2014) www.theguardian.com/world/2014/jan/21/australia-has-violated-timor-lestes-sovereignty-un-court-told (accessed 21 June 2015).

83 Anthony Aust, *Modern Treaty Law and Practice*, Cambridge: Cambridge University Press (2013), 6; Vienna Convention on the Law of Treaties (adopted on 22 May 1969, entered into force on 27 January 1980), 1155 UNTS 331 art. 1.

Oil Company case submitted to the court by the UK government in 1951 stated: "the text of the Iranian Declaration is not a treaty text resulting from negotiations between two or more states. It is the result of unilateral drafting by the Government of Iran, which appears to have shown a particular degree of caution when drafting the text of the Declaration."[84] Third, treaties should be concluded in written form, which excludes oral agreements. For a text to become a treaty, the Convention set out criteria that a treaty should be governed by international law. According to the International Law Commission's Commentary, the phrase "governed by international law" includes the element of "intention to create obligations under international law."[85] Apart from its name, a treaty employs terminology to create legal rights and obligations and expresses the intention of parties to create obligations under international law.

While concluding a treaty, states initiate several rounds of official meetings in order to express their terms and conditions and negotiate on those terms to find common ground. Good faith in negotiations and willingness to conclude a treaty is an international norm. According to D'Amato, the good faith principle requires parties to deal honestly and fairly, represent their motives truthfully, and refrain from taking unfair advantage.[86] Moreover, there are specific aspects of good faith as *pacta sund servanda*, abuse of rights and discretion, estoppel and acquiescence and negotiations in good faith.[87] Negotiations in good faith are applied well, especially for pre-contractual espionage activities.

The Vienna Convention obliged parties to perform treaties in good faith[88] and interpret treaties in good faith.[89] In addition, the ILC commentary extended the scope of good faith to the period of negotiations, stating, "in the case of treaties, there is the special consideration that the parties by negotiating and concluding the treaty have brought themselves into a relationship in which there are particular obligations of

84 Anglo-Iranian Oil Co. Case (*United Kingdom* v. *Iran*) (Preliminary Objection) [1951] www.icj-cij.org/docket/files/16/1997.pdf (accessed 21 June 2015), 105.
85 ILC, Draft Articles on the Law of Treaties with commentaries (1966) 189 http://legal. un.org/ilc/texts/instruments/english/commentaries/1_1_1966.pdf (accessed 21 June 2015).
86 Anthony D'Amato, "Good faith," in Rudolf Bernhardt (ed.), *Encyclopedia of Public International Law*, 7, Amsterdam: North Holland Publishing (1992), 108–09.
87 Steven Reinhold, "Good faith in international law," *UCL Journal of Law and Jurisprudence*, 2 (2013), Bonn Research Paper on Public International Law No. 2/ 2013 7.
88 Vienna Convention on the Law of Treaties (adopted on 22 May 1969, entered into force on 27 January 1980), 1155 UNTS 331 art. 26.
89 Ibid., art. 31.

good faith."[90] The question in this context is whether parties have an obligation to act in good faith in the creation of the rights and obligation. In the *Nuclear Tests* case, the ICJ put an end to this question and stated, "one of the principles governing the creation and performance of legal obligations, whatever their source, is the principle of good faith."[91] Apart from the Vienna Convention, the ICJ strictly underlined the principle of good faith in the *North Sea Continental Shelf* case. In this case, the court declared, "…they were to conduct themselves that the negotiations were meaningful."[92] Later on, in the *Fisheries Jurisdiction* case, the court underlined that the parties should conduct their negotiations based on good faith.[93] Furthermore, in the *Gabcikovo-Nagymaros Project* case, the ICJ stressed the significance of the good faith principle, especially in negotiations;

> Articles 65 to 67 of the Vienna Convention on the Law of Treaties, if not codifying customary law, at least generally reflect customary international law and contain certain procedural principles which are based on an obligation to act in good faith.[94]
>
> The obligations contained in Articles 15, 19 and 20 are, by definition, general and have to be transformed into specific obligations of performance through a process of consultation and negotiation. Their implementation thus requires a mutual willingness to discuss in good faith.[95]

In this regard, conducting cyberespionage or economic espionage activities in order to gain vastly superior bargaining power could result in bad faith, while negotiating to conclude a treaty. Therefore, such a treaty may be declared as void or invalid under the general principles of international law or customary law of treaties, even if it is signed. However, there is not any legal ground under the Vienna Convention for a failure to negotiate in good faith during negotiations for invoking a

---

90 International Law Commission, Draft Articles on the Law of Treaties with commentaries (1966), 262 http://legal.un.org/ilc/texts/instruments/english/commentaries/1_1_1966.pdf (accessed 21 June 2015).
91 ICJ, Nuclear Tests Case (*Australia* v. *France*) (Merits) (1974) para. 46.
92 ICJ, North Sea Continental Shelf Case (*Germany* v. *Denmark*; *Germany* v. *Netherlands*) (1969), 75 www.icj-cij.org/docket/files/52/5563.pdf.
93 ICJ, Fisheries Jurisdiction Case (*United Kingdom* v. *Iceland*) (Merits) (1974), 94 www.icj-cij.org/docket/files/55/5979.pdf (accessed 21 June 2015).
94 ICJ, Gabcikovo-Nagymaros Project (*Hungary* v. *Slovakia*) (1997), 63 www.icj-cij.org/docket/files/92/7375.pdf (accessed 21 June 2015).
95 Ibid., 68.

treaty as void or invalid. Thus, another legal ground should be adopted for invoking invalidity such as fraudulent conduct.

INVALIDITY OF TREATY BY FRAUD

The Vienna Convention devotes nine articles to invalidity, articles 46–53 and 64 cover provisions related to invalidity.[96] It is generally accepted that invalidity is rarely applicable.[97] According to article 49 of the Vienna Convention,

> If a State has been induced to conclude a treaty by the fraudulent conduct of another negotiating State, the State may invoke the fraud as invalidating its consent to be bound by the treaty.

Fraudulent conduct is not defined under the Vienna Convention. Article 49 purposely does not define fraud, because parties concluded that "it would be better to formulate the general concept of fraud applicable in the law of treaties in as clear terms as possible and to leave its precise scope to be worked out in practice and in the decisions of international tribunals."[98] However, the ILC commentary set out two descriptive elements for fraudulent conduct. These elements are fraudulent conduct and the intention to deceive.[99] According to the

---

96 Vienna Convention on the Law of Treaties (adopted on 22 May 1969, entered into force on 27 January 1980), 1155 UNTS 331.
97 Aust, *Modern Treaty Law and Practice*, 6: "even though the subject is no importance for the day-to-day work of a foreign ministry. The international Law Commission was well aware that invalidity was a rarity"; Mark E. Villiger, *Commentary on the 1969 Vienna Convention on the Law of Treaties*, Leiden: Martinus Nijhoff (2009), 617: "Fortunately, cases of fraud is rare in international law"; see Sinclair of the UK delegation, OR 1968 CoW 261, para. 24, "Article 49 might encourage States to invoke grounds of fraud more frequently."
98 Humprey Waldock, "Fifth Report on the Law of the Treaties," *Yearbook of the International Law Commission*, 2(11) (1965), para. 2 http://legal.un.org/ilc/publications/yearbooks/english/ilc_1966_v2.pdf (accessed 4 June 2018); see page 244: "Fraud is a concept found in most systems of law, but the scope of the concept is not the same in all systems. In international law, the paucity of precedents means that there is little guidance to be found either in practice or in the jurisprudence of international tribunals as to the scope to be given to the concept. In these circumstances, the Commission considered whether it should attempt to define fraud in the law of treaties. The Commission concluded, however, that it would suffice to formulate the general concept of fraud applicable in the law of treaties and to leave its precise scope to be worked out in practice and in the decisions of international tribunals."
99 André Oraison, "Le dol dans la conclusion des traités," *Revue Générale de Droit International*, 75 (1971), 630.

International Law Commission, the expression of "fraudulent conduct" is designed to include any false statements, misrepresentations
or other deceitful proceedings by which a state is induced to give consent to a treaty, which it would not otherwise have given.[100] The elements then appear as: (1) any false statements; (2) misrepresentations or
other deceitful proceedings. Article 49 assumes the fraudulent conduct
of another negotiating state. Fraud can only relate to conduct in the
making of a treaty during its negotiation and up to its conclusion, not
in its subsequent performance.[101]

Fraud is the antithesis of good faith.[102] The prohibition of fraud,
derived from good faith, which is a well-known principle in domestic
law, entered international law via general principles of international
law.[103] The definition of fraud in international law is much broader than
that found in domestic law.[104] It includes deliberately deceitful behavior
in the formation of an international agreement.[105] The Harvard Law
School's Draft Convention on the Law of Treaties from 1935 contained
a provision on fraud as well: "State which claims that it has been induced
to enter into a treaty with another State by the fraud of the latter State
may seek from a competent international tribunal or authority a declaration that the treaty is void."[106] It is also stated that this is a willful intent
to deceive another.[107]

Article 44 of the Convention regulates the separability of treaty
provisions:

> In cases falling under articles 49 and 50 the State entitled to invoke
> the fraud or corruption may do so with respect either to the whole
> treaty or, subject to paragraph 3, to the particular clauses alone.

---

100 ILC, Draft Articles on the Law of Treaties with commentaries (1966), 245 http://
legal.un.org/ilc/texts/instruments/english/commentaries/1_1_1966.pdf (accessed 21
June 2015).
101 Villiger, *Commentary*, 618; Statement in Vienna by the Italian delegation, OR 1968
CoW 262, para. 37.
102 Cheng Bin, *General Principles of Law as Applied by International Courts and
Tribunals*, Cambridge: Cambridge University Press (1953), 158.
103 Villiger, *Commentary*, 619.
104 Donald K. Anton, "Arbitrating the treaty on certain maritime arrangements in the
timor sea: espionage between neighbours in the latest round", ANU College of Law
Research Paper No. 13–20 (2013), 4.
105 Paul Reuter, *Introduction to the Law of Treaties*, New York: Routledge (1989),
137–38.
106 Supplement 1144. Article 31, para. (a) of the Harvard Draft.
107 Ibid.

In particular, in a case of alleged invalidity according to this provision, the ground of invalidity may be invoked only by the state which was the victim of the fraud or corruption;[108] and that state has the "permissive right"[109] either to invalidate the entire treaty or solely the particular clauses to which the fraud or corruption relate.[110] The paragraph gives the state, which was the victim of fraud or corruption, the possibility to choose between two different options: the option to invoke the invalidity of its consent either with respect to the whole treaty or with respect to particular clauses alone. This provision is based on the idea of favoring the injured state's party and sanctioning the state's party, which is held responsible for the fraud.[111]

However, there is a legal question as to whether espionage activities amount to "fraudulent conduct." According to Mitchell and Akande, "access to information in a treaty negotiation that was obtained through espionage may limit the parties' ability to negotiate freely and fairly," so such activities apparently become contrary to the principle of good faith and include deception.[112] Likewise, Anton includes espionage activities, which aim to obtain classified, confidential and privileged "information in order to gain an advantage in treaty negotiations is deceitful behavior."[113]

Cyberespionage or intelligence-gathering activities, due to their nature, are based on deception and carried out in order to for acquire a political, economic and technological advantage. In the case of negotiations, the outcome of espionage activities puts one of the parties in a well-informed position and creates information asymmetry, which certainly disrupts other parties' ability to negotiate. In this sense,

108 ILC Report 1966, *Yearbook of the International Law Commission*, 2(23) (1966), para. 6.
109 Statement by Waldock in the ILC, *Yearbook of the International Law Commission*, 1(226) (1963), para. 10.
110 Waldock Report V, ibid., 9, para. 5; the statement by Waldock in the ILC, *Yearbook of the International Law Commission*, 1(2) (1966), 318, para. 57 ("paragraph 4 simply provided two alternative courses for the State").
111 Oliver Dörr and Kirsten Schmalenbach, *Vienna Convention on the Law of Treaties: A Commentary*, Berlin: Springer (2012) 762–63.
112 Kate Mitchell and Dapo Akande, "Espionage & good faith in treaty negotiations: *East Timor v. Australia*," blog of *EJIL* (20 January 2014) www.ejiltalk.org/espionage-fraud-good-faith-in-treaty-negotiations-east-timor-v-australia-in-the-permanent-court-of-arbitration/ (accessed 27 July 2015).
113 Donald K. Anton, "The Timor sea treaty arbitration: Timor-Leste challenges Australian espionage and seizure of documents," *American Society of International Law*, 18(6) (2014) www.asil.org/insights/volume/18/issue/6/timor-sea-treaty-arbitration-timor-leste-challenges-australian-espionage (accessed 27 July 2015).

conducting espionage during negotiations can be categorized under fraudulent conduct and can constitute a legal base for invoking invalidity by fraud according to the Vienna Convention.

Legal responses to non-state cyberespionage

International law does not regulate or prohibit cyberespionage operations conducted by non-state actors or private entities. If such operations conducted by non-state actors can be attributed to any state, then measures explained earlier become applicable. States, as being a sole authority within their borders, should "exercise due diligence in not allowing its territory or cyber infrastructure under its governmental control to be used for cyber operations that affect the rights of, and produce serious consequences for, other states."[114] Within this context, first states should enact the necessary legislations to prevent such operations occurring within its territory. Second, if such an operation has been conducted from its territory, then the state should take further measures to prevent dissemination of the acquired information.

Furthermore, in certain circumstances, the targeted state might have a right to hack back.[115] Likewise, the International Group of Experts accepted that "responses directed against non-state actors may be permissible pursuant to the law of self-defense."[116]

TRIPS Agreement

Article 39 of the TRIPS Agreement requires Members of the WTO to provide protection of trade secrets against their unlawful acquisition, use or disclosure by third parties. Therefore, member states are obliged to implement the necessary regulations in their country. The lack of appropriate regulation in tackling the theft of trade secrets can trigger state responsibility.

There is no unitary law or approach dealing with trade secrets, in other words, the protection varies from member state to member state[117] and civil actions are adopted frequently against the misuse of trade

114 Schmitt, *Tallinn Manual 2.0*, 30, 175.
115 Manny Halberstam, "Hacking back: reevaluating the legality of retaliatory cyberattacks," *The George Washington International Law Review*, 46 (2013); Oğuz Kaan Pehlivan, "Siber saldırılar karşısında meşru müdafaa hakkı," *Kamu Hukuku Arşivi*, 17(1–2), *Adalet Yayınevi*, 2017.
116 Schmitt, *Tallinn Manual 2.0*, 175.
117 Joe Lang, "The protection of commercial trade secrets," *European Intellectual Property Review*, 25(10) (2003), 462.

secrets. In the late 1990s, criminalization of the misuse of trade secrets was proposed. The UK Law Commission consultation paper presents several arguments, which are embraced by other countries in support of criminalization of the misuse of trade secrets and breach of confidentiality.[118] According to the paper:

1. "there is no distinction in principle between the harm caused by such misuse and the harm caused by theft;
2. the imposition of legal sanctions is necessary in order to protect investment in research;
3. civil remedies alone are insufficient to discourage trade secret misuse (and would continue to be insufficient even if exemplary damages were made more widely available) because many wrongdoers are unable to satisfy any judgment against them;
4. it is inconsistent for the law to prohibit the infringement of copyright and registered trademarks but not the misuse of trade secrets; and
5. criminalization would help to preserve standards in business life."[119]

Nevertheless, even if the misuse of trade secrets is not criminalized that does not mean that perpetrators will escape criminal liability. For instance, "it is possible that the industrial spy, in the course of acquiring the trade secrets of another, might commit the criminal offense of burglary, or of gaining unauthorized access to a computer or of intercepting communication illegally."[120] In addition, a distinction is made in the legal literature between technical trade secrets and other trade secrets. Technical trade secrets concern information that is within patentable subjects, traditionally defined not to include business methods; non-technical trade secrets, on the other hand, refer to everything else, including the compilation of information and improved methods of organizing and conducting businesses.[121]

WTO dispute settlement mechanism

In accordance with the TRIPP and WTO agreements, states have an obligation to take necessary precautions to prevent occurring wrongful acquisition of trade secrets.

---

118 UK Law Commission, "Legislating the criminal code: misuse of trade secrets," *Law Commission Consultation Paper*, 15 (1997), 30.
119 Ibid.
120 Lang, "The protection of commercial trade secrets," 464.
121 Elizabeth A. Rowe and Sharon K. Sandeen, *Trade Secrecy And International Transactions Law and Practice*, Cheltenham: Edward Elgar Publishing (2015), 10.

"After decades of being ignored, trade secret rights have become a hot topic among international trade professionals and businesses alike. A primary driver of the increased attention is concerned about foreign and cyber-espionage."[122] Rowe and Sanden asserted that companies need more tools to combat such attacks and the institution of more effective trade secret laws is one possible solution. The TRIPS Agreement is an outcome of the Uruguay Round, the 8th round of multilateral trade negotiations conducted within the framework of the General Agreement on Tariffs and Trade (GATT), which continued from 1986 to 1994, in which 123 countries attended as contracting parties.[123]

After the publication of several reports underlining Chinese sophisticated cyberespionage campaigns, certain scholars have argued: "the victims of Chinese economic espionage should seek to establish clear guidelines and penalties within the World Trade Organization (WTO) system."[124] Indeed, in 2014, many US senators demanded US Trade Representatives initiate a case at the WTO against China for state-backed cyber espionage.[125] However, the US has not initiated a WTO complaint against China over this matter. The WTO is a global institution regulating trade negotiations in which WTO agreements cover goods, services and intellectual property, resolving disputes under the Dispute Settlement Understanding if the rights and obligations under the agreements infringed.[126] The WTO's Agreement on TRIPS has several articles about protection of intellectual property rights during the course of international trade. Article 39 of the TRIPS is the first time that protection of trade secrets has appeared in a multilateral treaty.[127] Article 39 set out principles to protect undisclosed information and trade secrets. According to the TRIPS:

122 Ibid., 15.
123 WTO, Overview: The TRIPS Agreement, accessed www.wto.org/egnlish/tratop_ e/trips/intel2_2.htm; for the detailed history of drafting TRIPS, see: Rochelle C. Dreyfuss and Katherine J. Strandburg (eds.), *The Law and Theory of Trade Secrecy: A Handbook of Contemporary Research*, Cheltenham: Edward Elgar Publishing (2011).
124 Richard Clarke, "A global cyber-crisis waiting to happen," *Washington Post* (7 February 2013) /www.washingtonpost.com/opinions/a-global-cyber-crisis-in-waiting/2013/02/ 07/812e024c-6fd6-11e2-ac36-3d8d9dcaa2e2_story.html (accessed 27 July 2015).
125 Brian T. Yeh, *Protection of Trade Secrets: Overview of Current Law and Legislation*, Washington, DC: Congressional Research Service (2016), 13 https://fas.org/sgp/crs/ secrecy/R43714.pdf (accessed 4 June 2018).
126 WTO, What We Do, www.wto.org/english/thewto_e/whatis_e/what_we_do_e.htm (accessed 27 July 2015).
127 Francois Dessemontet, "Arbitration and confidentiality," *American Review of International Arbitration*, 7 (1996), 307.

1. In the course of ensuring effective protection against unfair competition as provided in Article 10 bis of the Paris Convention (1967), Members shall protect undisclosed information in accordance with paragraph 2 and data submitted to governments or governmental agencies in accordance with paragraph 3.
2. Natural and legal persons shall have the possibility of preventing information lawfully within their control from being disclosed to, acquired by, or used by others without their consent in a manner contrary to honest commercial practices so long as such information:
    (a) is secret in the sense that it is not, as a body or in the precise configuration and assembly of its components, generally known among or readily accessible to persons within the circles that normally deal with the kind of information in question;
    (b) has commercial value because it is secret; and
    (c) has been subject to reasonable steps under the circumstances, by the person lawfully in control of the information, to keep it secret. [128]

Article 39(2) defines three requirements for information to be classified as undisclosed information or trade secrets. Article 39(2) states that information is protected if it: (a) is secret in the sense that it is not, as a body or in the precise configuration and assembly of its components, generally known among or readily accessible to persons within the circles that normally deal with the kind of information in question; (b) has commercial value because it is secret; and (c) has been subject to reasonable steps under the circumstances, by the person lawfully in control of the information, to keep it secret.

In this sense, article 39(2) did not give any definition about manners contrary to honest commercial practices, generally known, readily accessible, commercial value, etc., so it is left for the legislatures and courts of each country to identify the terms and acts, which are deemed dishonest.[129] However, footnote 10 to article 39/2 states that a manner contrary to honest commercial practices shall mean at least practices such as: (1) breach of contract, (2) breach of confidence, (3) inducement to breach and (4) the acquisition of undisclosed information by third parties who knew, or who were grossly negligent in failing to know

---

128 WTO, Agreement on Trade-Related Aspects of Intellectual Property Rights (adopted 15 April 1994, came into effect 1 January 1995) art. 39 www.wto.org/english/docs_e/legal_e/27-trips.pdf (accessed 27 July 2015).
129 Rowe and Sandeen, *Trade Secrecy*, 30.

that such practices were involved in the acquisition.[130] As in the commentary, "a manner contrary to honest commercial practices" has been explained as a "breach of contract, breach of confidence and inducement to breach, and includes the acquisition of undisclosed information by third parties who knew, or were grossly negligent in failing to know that such practices were involved in the acquisition."[131]

The WTO Agreement includes dispute settlement provisions that allow member states of the WTO to bring actions against other countries, which violate or are not in compliance with the terms of the WTO Agreement.[132] According to article 64 of the TRIPS, "the provisions of Articles XXII and XXIII of GATT 1994 as elaborated and applied by the Dispute Settlement Understanding shall apply to consultations and the settlement of disputes under this agreement except as otherwise specifically provided herein."[133] Therefore, any member states of the WTO, which do not comply with the provisions of article 39 of the TRIPS Agreement may bring forward the WTO Agreement's dispute settlement process.[134] The WTO dispute settlement system is codified in the Understanding on Rules and Procedures Governing the Settlement of Disputes.[135]

---

130 1) a contract that promises confidentiality, 2) an obligation not based upon a contract, 3) inducement of a breach of a duty to maintain secrecy, 4) referring to the previous three wrongful acts.

131 WTO, Agreement on Trade-Related Aspects of Intellectual Property Rights, 335.

132 Marrakesh Agreement Establishing the World Trade Organization, 15 April 1994. Dispute Settlement Understanding, Annex 2.

133 WTO, Agreement on Trade-Related Aspects of Intellectual Property Rights, article 64, 347.

134 Rufus Yerxa, "The power of the WTO dispute settlement system," in Rufus Yerxa and Bruce Wilson (eds.), *Key Issues in WTO Dispute Settlement*, Cambridge: Cambridge University Press (2005), 4: "The dispute settlement system works on the basis of contractual remedies. What this means is that the violation of WTO rules by one Member gives adversely affected Members the right to withdraw some equivalent value of commitments in order to rebalance their respective rights and obligations. Please note that I said it gives them the right! However, the decision to 'retaliate' is entirely up to the aggrieved Member itself, just as the decision to correct a violation rests on the sovereign decision of the violator. Thus, the dispute settlement process is merely a means of adjudicating whether a Member has acted contrary to its obligations, and if so, the extent to which other Members might be entitled to 'withdraw equivalent concessions' if the offending Member does not correct the violation. There are elaborate procedures designed to ensure that this 'right' they obtain from a WTO ruling is proportionate and fair. These are some of the basic realities one has to keep in mind when examining the WTO dispute settlement process. The WTO system works only to the extent Members want it to work, and only if they decide that compliance is in their overall economic interest. It therefore rests on the credibility of the rules, and also on the credibility of the dispute settlement decisions."

135 WTO, *A Handbook on the WTO Dispute Settlement System*, Cambridge: Cambridge University Press (2004), 17.

The WTO dispute settlement is a government-to-government procedure in which only WTO members themselves may invoke WTO rights and enforce WTO obligations against other members.[136] The WTO dispute settlement is a four-stage procedure consisting of a mandatory consultation stage, a panel stage, an appellate stage, and an implementation/compliance stage. In the mandatory 60-day consultation stage, the Complainant State should notify the other Member and the entire WTO membership of the nature of its complaint and any alleged violation of the WTO rule. If consultations fail, the complaining member may then request and is entitled to have its complaint heard by a panel normally composed of three, and exceptionally five, experts selected on an ad hoc basis.[137] If the panel finds that there are WTO violations, it recommends to the responding party to bring its disputed measures into conformity with its WTO obligations.

Panel proceedings are supposed to take no more than nine months.[138] Either party can appeal the panel report to the appellate body, which has 90 days to issue its own report. Pursuant to article 17, an appeal shall be limited to issues of law covered in the panel report and legal interpretations developed by the panel. The appellate body may uphold, modify or reverse the legal findings and conclusions of the panel.[139] Upon the completion of the appellate stage the appellate body, a report is adopted by the Dispute Settlement Body (DSB) and unconditionally accepted by the parties to the dispute unless the DSB decides by consensus not to adopt the appellate body report within 30 days following its circulation to the members. "Adoption by the DSB gives legal effect to the report or reports and a Member whose measures have been found in violation of its WTO obligations is expected to take such steps as necessary to bring the WTO-inconsistent measures into compliance with the relevant applicable WTO agreement."[140] However, cases relating to "undisclosed information" are rare and a complaint involving article 39 has occurred only once, and that case was eventually withdrawn after the

---

136 Bruce Wilson, "The WTO dispute settlement system and its operation: a brief overview of the first ten years," in Rufus Yerxa and Bruce Wilson (eds.), *Key Issues in WTO Dispute Settlement*, Cambridge: Cambridge University Press (2005) 16: "If a private actor from a WTO Member (e.g. a company, labor union, trade association, etc.) wishes to activate the WTO dispute settlement system against another WTO Member government, it must first persuade its own government to prosecute a complaint on its behalf against such other WTO Member."
137 WTO, *A Handbook*, 21.
138 Wilson, "The WTO dispute settlement," 17.
139 Annex 2 of the WTO Agreement, Understanding on rules and procedures governing the settlement of disputes (DSU), art. 17.
140 Wilson, "The WTO dispute settlement," 18.

parties (China and the European Communities) reached an agreement in the form of a Memorandum of Understanding.[141]

According to Fidler, obligations created by the WTO are only effective and binding not on the outside, but within the territories of the parties.[142] In other words, the targeted state should establish the link between the responsibility of the targeting state and economic cyberespionage. Moreover, Fidler believes that the WTO is not an appropriate forum to solve economic cyberespionage problems legally, but is appropriate to "put political pressure on States through this high-profile diplomatic forum."[143]

On the contrary, the preamble of the TRIPS Agreement stated the purpose of the agreement as to "reduce distortions and impediments to international trade ... and promote the effective and adequate protection of intellectual property rights."[144] From that point, Skinner underlined that cyber violations are within the limits of WTO agreements, and the interpretation of the preamble of the TRIPS Agreement enables the inclusion of economic cyberespionage operations within the agreement.[145]

In this sense, WTO litigation against the perpetrators of economic cyberespionage is another legal argument in relation to violations of treaty obligations and responsibility of states. Establishing the link between perpetrators of cyberespionage and violation of any rights and obligations under TRIPS is still lacking concrete legal argumentation. On the other hand, litigation in this field can be notoriously complicated and expensive, "particularly where highly technical trade secrets are involved and the defense alleges that the information the claimant seeks to protect is in fact widely known."[146] Moreover, article 39 of TRIPS stipulates and obliged every contracting party to enact appropriate domestic legal mechanisms for trade secret protection and

141 WTO, Dispute Settlement DS372, available at www.wto.org/english/tratop_e/dispu_e/cases_e/ds372_e.htm.
142 David P. Fidler, "Economic cyber espionage and international law: controversies involving government acquisition of trade secrets through cyber technologies," *ASIL*, 17(10) (2013) /www.asil.org/insights/volume/17/issue/10/economic-cyber-espionage-and-international-law-controversies-involving (accessed 15 July 2015).
143 David P. Fidler, "Why the WTO is not an appropriate venue for addressing economic cyber espionage," Arms Control Law Blog (11 February 2013) http://armscontrollaw.com/2013/02/11/why-the-wto-is-not-an-appropriate-venue-for-addressing-economic-cyber-espionage/ (accessed 27 July 2015).
144 WTO, Agreement on Trade-Related Aspects of Intellectual Property Rights (TRIPS) (adopted 15 April 1994), preamble.
145 Christina Parajon Skinner, "An international law response to economic cyber espionage," *Connecticut Law Review* 46 (2014), 1197.
146 Lang, "The protection of commercial trade secrets," 471.

the WTO regularly follows up whether those countries have sufficient protection mechanisms. Therefore even if we applied a literal interpretation for article 39, it is challenging to assert that solely this article is not sufficient to tackle with state to state cyberespionage operations. In other words, states can still initiate WTO a dispute settlement mechanism against states conducting cyberespionage, however, this process will be challenging for grounding illegality of such operations under existing WTO rules and especially TRIPS articles.

To this end, the WTO dispute resolution mechanism might be politically "the most appropriate and effective forum," but legally parties of the WTO and TRIPS should first agree on international norms and principles explicitly restricting economic cyberespionage operations under WTO agreements.

Comparative law responses

C.I.A, which stands for Confidentiality, Integrity, and Availability, is a key information security principle, which should be guaranteed by in any kind of secure system:[147] 1) Confidentiality is the ability to hide information from those people unauthorized to view it, 2) Integrity is the ability to ensure that data is an accurate and unchanged representation of the original secure information, 3) Availability is about the accessibility of the information concerned by an authorized viewer at all times.[148]

First, economic and industrial cyberespionage violates confidentiality, the integrity of a secured system and sometimes its availability. Therefore, states criminalize and punish any kind of violation of the above-mentioned principle. Confidentiality aims at the prevention of unauthorized disclosure of information. Regulations relating to the protection of trade and commercial secrets cover the confidentiality part. Integrity aims at ensuring that information is protected from unauthorized or unintentional alteration, modification or deletion. The integrity part is covered by regulations restricting any unauthorized access to a computer or a secure network.

Espionage activities are regulated through domestic legal systems all over the world. These activities are described under criminal codes where various punishments such as imprisonment and fines are

---

147 Y. Feruza Sattarova and Prof. Tao-hoon Kim, "IT security review: privacy, protection, access control, assurance and system security," *International Journal of Multimedia and Ubiquitous Engineering*, 2(2) (2007), 18–19.
148 Oğuz Kaan Pehlivan, "Siber dünya: gerçekler ve reel tehditler," *Analist Journal*, 31 (2013), 62.

stipulated. It is significant to be aware that tools enabling espionage have changed fundamentally over a decade as detailed in the previous chapter. In this sense, existing legal documents and provisions covering espionage are designed and enacted at a time when human-based intelligence is prioritized. However, today's business environment is profoundly different from the 1990s. Therefore, new rules and crimes have been developed and enacted for preventing cyberespionage operations. In general, domestic regulations provide trade secret protection and cyber crimes as legal mechanisms to tackle cyberespionage.

Turkish legal system

There is not any specific regulation on economic and industrial cyberespionage under the Turkish legal system. However, provisions relating to the protection of trade secrets, especially with unauthorized access and interception, have covered cyberespionage activities as well. Therefore, we will examine these provisions and their relation to prevention of cyberespionage activities.

Protection of trade secrets

There is not any specific law or legislation in effect regarding trade secrets and their protection. However, in Turkish legal literature, it is acknowledged that several requirements/conditions have to exist for information or documents to be considered as a trade secret. According to the Usluel, confidentiality and having commercial value makes commercial information or knowledge a trade secret.[149] The confidentiality feature of a trade secret should be considered as such information that should not be known by other rivals operating in the same industry, the owner of the trade secret should take appropriate measures to protect that secret, and finally, the trade secret should not be acquired legally.[150] According to Öztek, a trade secret is "any undisclosed information related to a commercial entity's business and that is intentionally kept secret by its owner, which creates a commercial advantage for its owner in terms of competition and have an independent commercial value."[151] The generally accepted main conditions of trade secrets are: 1) a trade

---

149 Aslı E. Gürbüz Usluel, *Anonim Şirketlerde Ticari Sırrın Korunması*, İstanbul: Vedat (2009), 29.
150 Ibid., 32–38.
151 Selçuk Öztek, "Protection of trade secrets through ipr and unfair competition law," *AIPPIA* Yearbook Vol. 3 (2010), 3.

secret is to be non-disclosed information, 2) a trade secret must have commercial value, 3) the information should be secret and 4) the owner of the information should have the intention not to disclose the relevant information.[152]

Additionally, the Court of Cassation stated, "the most significant features of trade secrets are being confidential and unknown by society or other colleagues or enterprises in the same sector."[153] Along with this requirement, a trade secret "must not be generally/publicly known. Secondly, the owner of the secret must be aware of the value of this information and willing to keep it confidential. Finally, the secret must be based on real facts, persons or information."[154] In other words, a trade secret should possess such qualities as the existence of confidential information, the will to keep it secret, the interest of the owner in keeping it secret and veracity. There is a long-awaited draft law on trade secrets, banking secrets and client secrets, which is now before the Parliamentary Commission. The draft law gives the definition of a trade secret as:

> the information and documents relating to the field of operations of a commercial enterprise or company, those are and that can be known and acquired only by a specific number of members and other officials that are exposed to the risk of the emergence of losses particularly if they are learned by the rivals and that should not be disclosed to the third parties that are extremely vital for the enterprise and for the success and efficiency in the economic life of the company, that contain important information internal structure or organization of enterprise, its financial, economic, credit and cash status, its research and development studies, its operation strategy, its resources for raw materials, the technical characteristics of productions, its pricing policies, its marketing tactics and expenses, its market share, its client potential and client networks on wholesale and retail sale basis, as well as its contractual contacts for items are subject to permission and that are not subject to permission and other relevant information and documents.

The draft law listed several types of trade secrets such as: organizational structure, financial and cash position, creditworthiness, research

---

152 Ibid., 4.
153 Yargıtay, 11. HD., E.2004/7827; K.2007/5755.
154 Uğur Aktekin and Deniz Doğan Alkan, "Trade secret protection Turkey chapter," in Trevor Cook (ed.), *Trade Secret Protection: A Global Guide*, London: Globe Law and Business (2016), 418.

and development activities, activity strategies, raw material resources, employee information, technical details of a means of production, pricing policies, marketing tactics and costs, market shares, connected retailers and wholesalers, customer lists and information, contractual links, databases and working methods. However, these are examples provided for illustration and do not comprise an exhaustive list.

Although there is not any specific regulation on trade secrets, Turkish law offers civil and criminal remedies in case of the violations of trade secrets.

CIVIL REMEDIES

The main legal instrument for addressing violations of trade secrets is the "unfair competition" provisions of the Turkish Commercial Code (TCC). Unfair competition is regulated under chapter 4 (from article 54 to article 63) of the TCC, No. 6103 (TCC).[155] Article 54 states: "1) purpose of the provisions regarding unfair competition is to create, for the benefit of all participants, a just and undamaged competition, 2) acts or commercial practices which are deceptive or in any other manner against good faith affecting the relationship between competitors or between the suppliers and customers are unfair and against the law." Article 55 listed acts against good faith and commercial practices: subsection (d) states that acquiring business secrets without permission constitute unfair competition. The wording of the article is as follows: "to divulge manufacturing and business secrets illegally, especially one who utilizes and makes known to other information and business secrets of a manufacturer which he has acquired secretly and without permission or in any other illegal manner shall be acting against goodwill."[156]

---

155 Turkish Commercial Code with n.6102 (accepted on 13 January 2011, Official Gazette No. 27846 dated on 14 February 2011).
156 Ibid. The unfair competition cases set forth under the above-mentioned article do not have a numerus clausus limitation. Article 55 listed out acts against good faith and commercial practices as:
   (a) Advertisements and sales methods against good faith and other unlawful acts;
   (b) To direct to infringe or to terminate an agreement;
   (c) To benefit from others' business products without authorization;
   (d) To divulge manufacturing and business secrets illegally, in particular, one who utilizes and makes known to others information and business secrets of a manufacturer which he has acquired secretly and without permission or in any other illegal manner shall be acting against goodwill.
   (e) Not to abide by the rules of business; in particular persons who do not abide by the business rules which have been set as a responsibility of his competitors as well

Pursuant to article 56, anyone who, through unfair competition, suffers injury as regards his customers, his credit, his professional reputation, his commercial activities or other economic interests or is exposed to such a danger may demand:

(a) the establishment of the unfairness of the act;
(b) the prevention of unfair competition;
(c) the suppression of the material conditions resulting from unfair competition and, if unfair competition rests on untrue or deceitful statements, the rectification of these statements;
(d) compensation of losses and damages, if there is a fault;
(e) payment of moral damages in case of the existence of the circumstances indicated in Article 58 of the Law of Obligations. The judge may, as damages in favor of the plaintiff and in accordance with the provision of paragraph (d), also order the equivalent of the advantages which the defendant might secure through unfair competition.

In other words, the right owner can ask through the court for the violations to be determined, stopped and prevented, request an interlocutory injunction, request the restitution of the material status/facts resulting from the unfair competition, and payment of compensation for material and moral damages sustained because of the violations.

Article 63 of the TCC held liable legal entities if an act of unfair competition has been committed during the performance of such legal entities' work. In case the unfair competition act is committed within the frame of a legal entity's activities, application of cautionary measures special to such legal entities may also be ruled. The trade secrets obtained by means of fraud, espionage or the provisions of TCC cover other improper means and there are no limitations as to the remedies in such cases.[157]

CRIMINAL REMEDIES

Criminal remedies for accessing trade secrets illegally are regulated under the Turkish Penal Code (TPC).[158] Disclosure of business secrets,

through a law or an agreement or who do not abide by the business rules common in a profession branch or a business environment shall be acting against goodwill.
(f) To use transactional conditions that are against goodwill; in particular persons who use previously written transactional conditions against the other party in a deceiving manner.

157 Öztek, "Protection of trade secrets," 8.
158 Turkish Criminal Code, Law Nr. 5237 (passed on 26 September 2004, Official Gazette No. 25611 dated 12 October 2004).

banking secrets log or information relating to customers are punishable activities according to the TPC.

Article 239 of the Penal Code states that persons holding information or documents containing commercial secrets, banking secrets or client secrets because of their job or job title, who are then found, upon complaint, to have disclosed the information or documents to unauthorized persons, are liable to be sentenced to imprisonment from one to three years and to have a judicial fine.[159] The persons who obtain the information and documents through unlawful means and give or disclose them to unauthorized persons will be sentenced likewise. If these secrets are disclosed to a foreigner residing abroad or his officers, the penalty will be increased by one third of the principal penalty.

The subsection above widens the scope of this article through scientific researches, discoveries or industrial practices. Pursuant to the first two subsections, persons who unlawfully acquired this information or documents and delivered or disclosed this information or documents to unauthorized individuals are also defined as offenders. In addition to that, if persons who unlawfully acquired such information/documents deliver or disclose these secrets to foreigners or their personnel domiciled outside of Turkey, punishment to be imposed is increased by one third. In the case that a trade secret has been acquired through computer network operations, this unauthorized access is separately punishable under the TPC.

---

159 It is estimated that the judicial fine may correspond to up to 5,000 days at a rate of 20 TL to 100 TL per day, according to the decision of judge in the case.

1. Any person who delivers information or documents which he holds by virtue of office about the customers, or discloses business secrets, banking secrets log is sentenced to imprisonment from one year to three years and also imposed a punitive fine up to five thousand days upon complaint. In case of delivery or disclosure of this information or documents to unauthorized individuals by the persons who unlawfully acquired such information/documents, the offender is punished according to the provision of this subsection.

2. Provisions of the first subsection are applicable also for the information relating to scientific researches or discoveries or industrial practices.

3. Punishment to be imposed is increased by one third in case of disclosure of these secrets to the foreigners or their personnel domiciled outside of Turkey. In that case, no complaint is sought.

4. Any person who leads another person to disclose the information or documents within the scope of this article by using force or threat is punished with imprisonment from three years to seven years.

Cyber crimes

UNAUTHORIZED ACCESS

Given the fact that almost every bit of business, legal and personal information has been digitalized, it is acknowledged that crime can be committed through digital platforms and tailored tools for accessing such information. Therefore, the TPC has special provisions on unauthorized access to data processing systems. The article 243 gives details of the crime and stipulates appropriate punishment.[160]

Within this article, unlawfully or unauthorized access to a part or whole of a network becomes punishable, without any condition such as to acquire the data within that network.[161] Therefore, this crime has been committed when unauthorized access has happened. Similarly, the Court of Cassation ruled: "suspect was accused of accessing a commercial bank account while he did not make any transaction using this system. Therefore, it is contrary to the law, ruling in accordance with the article 243/4 while disregarding article 243/1."[162]

According to the first subsection, the *actus reus* element of this crime consists of "unlawfully access" and "remaining" activities. The term "remaining" covers APT. The *means rea* element of this crime is accessing and remaining activities should be done intentionally. In addition, the recently enacted fourth subsection stipulates an imprisonment from one to three years for anyone who unlawfully traces data transmissions with technical devices in a data processing system, or between data processing systems, without having authorization.

160 Turkish Criminal Code, Law Nr. 5237 (passed on 26 September 2004, Official Gazette No. 25611 dated 12 October 2004). Article 243:

1. Any person who unlawfully enters a part or whole of data processing systems or remains there is punished with imprisonment up to one year, or imposed punitive fine.
2. In case the offenses defined in above subsection involve systems which are benefited against charge, the punishment to be imposed is increased up to one half.
3. If such act results with deletion or alteration of data within the content of the system, the person responsible from such failure is sentenced to imprisonment from six months up to two years.
4. Any person who unlawfully traces data transmissions with technical devices in a data processing system or between data processing systems without accessing the system, is punished with imprisonment from one year to three years.

161 Murat Volkan Dülger, *Bilişim Suçları ve Internet İletişim Hukuku*, İstanbul: Seçkin (2012), 313.
162 Yargıtay, 11. C.D., 26.03.2009, E.2008/18190 K. 2009/3058.

Article 244 of the TPC states a crime for hindrance or destruction of the system, deletion or alteration of data within that system. According to the article, any person who hinders or destroys operations of a data processing system; any person who garbles, deletes, changes or prevents access to data, or installs data in the system or sends the available data to other places are punishable.[163]

Pursuant to article 246(4), security precautions specific to legal entities are imposed in the case of commission of the offenses listed in this section and within the frame of activities or benefit of legal entities. Therefore, in cases of conviction of a crime through the participation of the organs or representatives of a legal entity, security precautions stipulated under article 60 become applicable. As a security precaution, the court may decide on the cancellation of an authorization license or confiscation of their property.

ILLEGAL INTERCEPTION OF DATA AND SYSTEMS

Intercepting communication network and traffic data is prohibited under the Turkish Constitution and TPC. According to article 22 of the Turkish Constitution, in regulating freedom of communication it is accepted that:

Everyone has the freedom of communication.

Privacy of communication is fundamental. Unless there exists a decision duly given by a judge on one or several of the grounds of national security, public order, prevention of crime, protection of public health and public morals, or protection of the rights and freedoms of others, or unless there exists a written order of an

---

163 Turkish Criminal Code, Law Nr. 5237 (passed on 26 September 2004, Official Gazette No. 25611 dated 12 October 2004). Article 244:

1. Any person who hinders or destroys operation of a data processing system is punished with imprisonment from one year to five years.
2. Any person who garbles, deletes, changes or prevents access to data, or installs data in the system or sends the available data to other places is punished with imprisonment from six months to three years.
3. The punishment to be imposed is increased by one half in case of commission of these offenses on the data processing systems belonging to a bank or credit institution, or public institutions or corporations.
4. Where the execution of above-mentioned acts does not constitute any other offense apart from unjust benefit secured by a person for himself or in favor of third parties, the offender is sentenced to imprisonment from two years to six years, and also imposed punitive fine up to five thousand days.

agency authorized by law in cases where delay is prejudicial, again on the above-mentioned grounds, communication shall not be impeded nor its privacy be violated. The decision of the competent authority shall be submitted for the approval of the judge having jurisdiction within twenty-four hours. The judge shall announce his decision within forty-eight hours from the time of the seizure; otherwise, seizure shall be automatically lifted.

Criminal Code under section 9 regulates the offenses against privacy and secrecy of life. Pursuant to article 132, any person who violates the confidentiality of communication between persons; any person who unlawfully publicizes the contents of a communication between persons; any person who unlawfully discloses the content of a communication between himself and others without obtaining their consent will be punished.[164]

In the case of commission of the offenses defined in the above article, the punishment is increased by one half, if the offense is committed by abusing his or her position or profession. Moreover, security precautions specific to legal entities are imposed in cases of commission of offenses, defined in the above articles, by legal entities.

In addition to that, law no. 6698, regarding Personal Data Protection, was enacted and published in the Official Gazette.[165] Article 30 of the law envisaged certain provisions to be amended and new provisions to be added. In this context, article 243/4 of the TPC reported: "monitoring data transfers which occurs within an information system or between information systems by technical tools without entering the system is

---

164 Turkish Criminal Code, Law Nr. 5237 (passed on 26 September 2004, Official Gazette No. 25611 dated 12 October 2004). Article 132:

1. Any person who violates the confidentiality of communication between persons shall be sentenced to a penalty of imprisonment of a term of 1 to 3 years. If the violation of confidentiality occurs through the recording of the content of the communication, the penalty to be imposed shall be increased by one fold.

2. Any person who unlawfully publicizes the contents of a communication between persons shall be sentenced to a penalty of imprisonment for a term of 2 to 5 years.

3. Any person who unlawfully discloses the content of a communication between himself and others without obtaining their consent shall be sentenced to a penalty of imprisonment for a term of 1 to 3 years. (Sentence added on 2 July 2012 – by Article 79 of the Law no. 6352) *Where such conversation is published in the press or broadcasted, the penalty to be imposed shall be the same.*

165 Turkish Law on Personal Data Protection with Nr.6698 (accepted on 24 March 2016 Official Gazette No. 29677 dated on 7 April 2016).

punishable by 1 to 3 years of imprisonment." The purpose of this article is to punish illegal monitoring and interception.

Likewise, the articles of the Wassenaar Arrangement regulate and restrict the trade of intrusion and surveillance items, as in article 245/A/1 of the TPC, which regulates prohibited devices and programs. According to article 245/A/1, "creating or producing a device, computer program, password or other security code for committing a crime and individuals who manufacture, import, deliver, convey, store, accept, sell, prepare them to be sold, deliver to others or who owned them shall be punished by one to three years of imprisonment or judicial fine up to five thousand days."

The provisions above are not specifically designed to answer the rising problem of intrusions and espionage, but these are available tools designed for combating cyberespionage. Nevertheless, despite being stipulated and applied under domestic legislations, these provisions contribute to ease the mutual legal assistance process and other kind of cooperation between law enforcement and judiciary officials regarding the cross-border nature of cyber attacks and activities related to cyberespionage.

American legal system

Under the American legal system, economic and industrial cyberespionage is subject to criminal and civil remedies. The Economic Espionage Act of 1996 is *lex specialis* and the primary legal mechanism to tackle cyberespionage. This act criminalizes certain economic and industrial espionage acts with penalties up to 10 years. Along with the Espionage Act, the US legal system regulates theft of trade secrets, and the Computer Fraud and Abuse Act of 1986 criminalizes unauthorized access to a computer or network.

Along with the above-mentioned wrongful acquisition of trade secrets, the American legal system stipulates civil remedies as a trade secret misappropriation.

Economic and industrial espionage

Contrary to the Turkish legal system, the US Economic Espionage Act of 1996 ("the Act") gives detailed definitions of economic and industrial espionage.[166] The Act criminalizes two kinds of activities – the theft

---

166 Economic Espionage Act 1996 sec 101, 18 USC § 1831–1839.

of trade secrets[167] to benefit a foreign actor[168] and theft for commercial or economic purposes.[169] Each crime is subject to different penalties and fines.

According to the Act, economic espionage occurs when someone is intending or knows that the offense will benefit any foreign government, foreign instrumentality, or foreign agent, knowingly: (1) steals, or without authorization appropriates, carries away, conceals, or obtains by deception or fraud a trade secret; (2) copies, duplicates, reproduces, destroys, uploads, downloads, or transmits that trade secret without authorization; or (3) receives a trade secret knowing that the trade secret had been stolen, appropriated, obtained or converted without authorization.

Industrial espionage occurs when someone knows that his or her offense will injure the owner of a trade secret of a product produced for or placed in interstate or foreign commerce, or acts with the intent to convert that trade secret to the economic benefit of anyone other than the owner by: (1) stealing, or without authorization appropriating, carrying away, concealing, or obtaining by deception or fraud information related to that secret; (2) copying, duplicating, reproducing, destroying, uploading, downloading, or otherwise transmitting that information without authorization; or (3) receiving that information knowing that that information had been stolen, appropriated, obtained or converted without authorization.[170]

According to those definitions, the *mens rea* element for this crime is intending or knowing whether his or her action will benefit any foreign government or will injure the owner of a trade secret. The *actus reus* element for committing this crime is acquiring trade secrets to the economic benefit of anyone other than the owner.

---

167 According to Economic Espionage Act, "trade secret" means all forms and types of financial, business, scientific, technical, economic or engineering information, including patterns, plans, compilations, program devices, formulas, designs, prototypes, methods, techniques, processes, procedures, programs, or codes, whether tangible or intangible, and whether or how stored, complied, or memorialized physically, electronically, graphically, photographically or in writing, if

    (A) the owner thereof has taken reasonable measures to keep such information secret; and

    (B) the information derives independent economic value, actual or potential, from being generally known to and not being readily ascertainable through proper means by public.

168 Ibid., 18 U.S.C. § 1831(a).
169 Ibid., 18 U.S.C. § 1832.
170 Economic Espionage Act 1996 sec 101, 18 USC § 1832.

The Act also defines foreign powers/actors, or "foreign instrumentality," as any agency, bureau, ministry, component, institution, association or any legal, commercial or business organization, corporation, firm or entity that is substantially owned, controlled, sponsored, commanded, managed or dominated by a foreign government. The Economic Espionage Act penalizes any above-mentioned activities if a foreign power/actor gains benefit from them. According to the US Code § 1839 3: "the term 'foreign agent' means any officer, employee, proxy, servant, delegate, or representative of a foreign government." Regarding economic espionage, "benefit means not only economic benefit but also reputational, strategic, or tactical benefit."[171] There is a distinction made between individuals and organizations.[172] Individuals who commit this crime will be subject to 15 years' imprisonment or a five million USD fine. In cases of organizations, there is not any imprisonment, but the fine will not be greater than 10 million USD or three times the value of the stolen trade secret.

Although it is rarely applicable, the Act was applied in May 2014 against five Chinese military hackers responsible for economic espionage. This was the first ever case filed against state actors. Grand Jury of Western District of Pennsylvania (WDPA) indicted the hackers with allegations;

1.　…conspired to hack into American entities, to maintain unauthorized access to their computers and to steal information from those entities that would be useful to their competitors in China, including state-owned enterprises (SOEs)
2.　…stole trade secrets that would have been particularly beneficial to Chinese companies at the time they were stolen
3.　…stole sensitive, internal communications that would provide a competitor, or an adversary in litigation, with insight into the strategy and vulnerabilities of the American entity.[173]

In the indictment, it is stated, "the conspirators trade secrets that would have been particularly beneficial to Chinese companies at the time they

171　Charles Doyle, *Stealing Trade Secrets and Economic Espionage: An Overview of 18 U.S.C. 1831 and 1832*, Washington, DC: Congressional Research Service (2014), 11 www.fas.org/sgp/crs/secrecy/R42681.pdf (accessed 4 June 2018).
172　Title 18 U.S.C., Section 1831 Economic Espionage.
173　Department of Justice, US Charges Five Chinese Military Hackers for Cyber Espionage Against US Corporations and a Labor Organization for Commercial Advantage (19 May 2014) www.justice.gov/opa/pr/us-charges-five-chinese-military-hackers-cyber-espionage-against-us-corporations-and-labor (accessed 4 June 2018).

were stolen."[174] According to the indictment, "conspirators also stole sensitive, internal communications that would provide a competitor, or adversary in litigation, with insight into the strategy and vulnerabilities of the American entity."[175] The attackers alleged to steal "1.4 gigabytes of data, the equivalent of roughly 700,000 pages of e-mail messages and attachments" from Westinghouse's computers between 2010 and 2012.[176] Westinghouse is a civilian nuclear power plant developer and constructor, and at that time, they were constructing a nuclear power plant in China. Similarly, US Steel, the largest steel company in the US, was targeted when it had significant business interests with China. While the company was participating in several international trade disputes with Chinese steel manufacturers, 1,753 US Steel computers were infiltrated by spear-phishing e-mails.

Trade secret protection

Under the US legal system, trade secrets are protected under state law, which differs from state to state. Most of the states have enacted a trade secret law, although some of them rely on common principles. In this regard, the Uniform Trade Secrets Act 1985 (UTSA) has created a uniform body of law.[177] Forty-eight states and the District of Columbia have enacted the same version of theUTSA.[178] While New York and

174 *United States* v. *Wang Dong, Sun Kai Liang, Wen Xinyu, Huang Zhenyu, Gu Chunhi*, Criminal No. 14–118, District Court West District of Pennsylvania (1 May 2014) www.justice.gov/iso/opa/resources/5122014519132358461949.pdf (accessed 4 June 2018).
175 Ibid., 3.
176 Ibid., 16.
177 Uniform Trade Secrets Act With 1985 Amendments www.wipo.int/edocs/lexdocs/laws/en/us/us034en.pdf (accessed 4 June 2018).
178 Susan Hargrove and Kayla Marshall, *The Prospect of a Federal Trade Secret Claim*, North Carolina: Smith Anderson Law Firm, 2 April 2015 www.smithlaw.com/resources-publications-Trade-Secret-Claim (accessed 10 January 2018); see also Uniform Law Commission, Legislative Fact Sheet - Trade Secrets Act www.uniformlaws.org/LegislativeFactSheet.aspx?title=Trade%20Secrets%20Act (accessed 4 June 2018). States enacted the UTSA: Alabama, Alaska, Arizona, Arkansas, California, Colorado, Connecticut, Delaware, District of Columbia, Florida, Georgia, Hawaii, Idaho, Illinois, Indiana, Iowa, Kansas, Kentucky, Louisiana, Maine, Maryland, Michigan, Minnesota, Mississippi, Missouri, Montana, Nebraska, Nevada, New Hampshire, New Jersey, New Mexico, North Dakota, Ohio, Oklahoma, Oregon, Pennsylvania, Puerto Rico, Rhode Island, South Carolina, South Dakota, Tennessee, Texas, US Virgin Islands, Utah, Vermont, Virginia, Washington, West Virginia, Wisconsin, Wyoming.

Massachusetts rely upon common law principles, North Carolina has implemented a modified version of the UTSA.

THEFT OF A TRADE SECRET-WRONGFUL ACQUISITION

Although it is commonly referred to as industrial espionage, the US legal system has separate provisions to regulate the theft of trade secrets. A trade secret is defined under the UTSA as;

> information, including a formula, pattern, compilation, program device, method, technique, or process, that: (i) derives independent economic value, actual or potential, from no being generally known to, and not being readily ascertainable by proper means by, other persons who can obtain economic value from its disclosure or use, and (ii) is the subject of efforts that are reasonable under the circumstances to maintain its secrecy.

Therefore, one of the key elements of the crime is that the trade secret should derive "independent economic value ... from not being generally known to ... the public." In the case of *Lansig Linde Ltd.* v. *Kerr*, it is argued that trade secrets are defined as:

> What are trade secrets and how do they differ (if at all) from confidential information? Mr. Poulton suggested that a trade secret is information, which, if disclosed to a competitor, would be liable to cause real or significant harm to the owner of the secret. I would add first that it must be information used in a trade or business, and secondly that the owner must limit the dissemination of it or at least not encourage or permit widespread publication.[179]

According to Toren, the definition given by the UTSA sets a minimal standard and courts have held information, which affords only a slight advantage to the holder, and which may qualify as a trade secret.[180] To illustrate, in *Sheridan* v. *Mallinckrodt, Inc.* case, the court stated that "although the advantages of a trade secret may be slight, they are responsible for helping to control production costs, and do, therefore provide the owner with a competitive edge (advantage)."[181] The court can adopt numerous

179 *Lansig Linde Ltd* v. *Kerr*, Weekly Law Report 1 (1991), 251.
180 Peter J. Toren, *Intellectual Property and Computer Crimes*, New York: Law Journal Press (2016), Chapter 5, 17.
181 *Sheridan* v. *Mallinckrodt, Inc.*, 568 F. Supp. 1347, US District Court for the Northern District of New York – 568 F. Supp. 1347 (N.D.N.Y 1983).

methods to prove the existence of a competitive edge (advantage) that trade secret may provide to the owner. In the *United States* v. *Bottone* case, the court ruled that the "value of these papers (stolen formulas) ... secret processes for which European drug manufacturers were willing to pay five and six figures."[182] Calculation of the independent economic value of the information may be based on open market indicators or the court may use a "thieves' market" as a proper means of valuing stolen goods or property. The court allows the use of a thieves' market and ruled that "the valuation of stolen goods according to the concept of a thieves' market is an appropriate method for determining the market value of goods."[183]

In some respects, collecting intelligence in the market place is essential for companies to survive. For instance, as legally grounded in the *Mars UK Ltd* v. *Teknowledge Ltd* case,[184] purchasing a competitor's product and analysis of that product through reverse engineering is plausible. However, in a case of industrial espionage, the US Court of Appeals concluded that aerial photographing of a plant under construction is "an improper method[185] of discovering the trade secrets."[186]

Pursuant to the Act, the theft of trade secrets is (1) whoever knowingly performs targeting or acquisition of trade secrets or (2) intends to convert a trade secret to knowingly benefit anyone other than the owner. This indicates the *means rea* element of the crime. On the other hand, the *actus reus* element of this crime is defined as to (1) steal, conceal, or carry away by fraud, artifice, or deception; (2) copy, duplicate, sketch, draw, photographs, download, upload, alter, destroy, photocopy, replicate, transmit, deliver, send, mail, communicate, or convey; (3) receive, buy, or possess a trade secret, knowing the same to have been stolen or appropriated, obtained, or converted without authorization.

---

182 *United States* v. *Caesar Bottone, Seymour Salb, and Nathan Sharff*, 365 F.2d 389 (2d Circuit 1966).

183 *United States* v. *Michael J. Oberhard*, No. 89–1503. United States Court of Appeals, Seventh Circuit (1989); *United States* v. *Stegora*, 849 F.2d 291, 292 (8th Circuit 1988).

184 *Mars UK Ltd* v. *Teknowledge Ltd*, Fleet Street Reports 18, Sweet and Maxwell (1999).

185 Under the Trade Secret Law of most of the states in US defines "improper means" includes theft, bribery, misrepresentation, breach or inducement of a breach of a duty to maintain secrecy, or espionage through electronic or other means. Reverse engineering or independent derivation alone shall not be considered improper means (Trade Secret Law California).

186 *E. I Du Pont de Nemours & Company* v. *Rolfe Christoper*, No. 28254 (US Court of Appeals, 5th Circuit) (1970).

In 2012, the High Court narrowed the jurisdictional scope of the act in the *United States* v. *Aleynikov* case.[187] The Court interpreted the wording of the provision, as per the Economic Espionage Act, as only applicable to the trade secret if it relates to products that a company sells and not those related to products that a company uses internally. A year later, the Theft of Trade Secrets Clarification Act was enacted. This act amended the scope of the Economic Espionage Act to include trade secrets related to "a product or service used in or intended for use" in commerce.[188]

Unlike economic espionage, the beneficiary of the theft of trade secrets must be anyone other than the owner of the misappropriated trade secrets. The maximum sentence for individuals who committed the theft is 10 years' imprisonment, 250,000 USD or an alternative fine based on gain/loss figures. In the case of committing the crime through an organization, there is only a maximum five million USD organizational fine.[189]

Theft of trade secrets involves the intent to harm the owner, however, an intent to benefit a foreign actor/power or a knowledge of that result is required for economic espionage. Economic espionage encloses all trade secrets "notwithstanding the absence of any connection to interstate or foreign commerce."[190] Therefore, imprisonment and fines are more severe compared to the theft of trade secrets.

In addition to that, there are ongoing negotiations on free trade agreements between the US and (1) the Trans-Pacific Partnership (TPP), which involves 11 countries in the Asia-Pacific region, and (2) the Transatlantic Trade and Investment Partnership (TTIP) with the European Union. According to the US Chamber of Commerce,

> Some TPP countries, such as Canada, Australia, Malaysia, and Singapore, have no laws criminalizing traditional trade secret disclosure or misappropriation. Many of these countries have criminal laws targeting computer-related crimes, which may sweep some forms of trade secret infringement into their purview but do not address trade secrets directly. Among those countries that do

187 *United States* v. *Aleynikov*, No. 11–1126 (2d Circuit 2012).
188 Warrington Parker, "President Obama signs into law the Theft of Trade Secrets Clarification Act," Orrick News Alert, 1 March 2013, accessed www.orrick.com/Events-and-Publications/Pages/President-Obama-Signs-into-Law-the-Theft-of-Trade-Secrets-Clarification-Act.aspx (accessed 4 June 2018).
189 Title 18 U.S.C., Section 1832 Theft of Trade Secrets.
190 Doyle, *Stealing Trade Secrets and Economic Espionage*, 8.

criminalize trade secret misappropriation or disclosure, the penalties often vary from those that would not provide sufficient deterrent effect to those that would but only if applied consistently ... The low criminal penalties or lack thereof in some TPP jurisdictions are particularly troublesome, as criminal penalties are believed to provide a greater deterrent to the trade secret thief than the prospect of a civil penalty alone.[191]

The report of the US Chamber of Commerce shows that states should enact appropriate laws to improve trade secret protection. Therefore, harmonization efforts for criminal laws penalizing the wrongful acquisition of trade secrets are significant.

TRADE SECRET MISAPPROPRIATION

The UTSA Section 1. (2) gives a definition of trade secret misappropriation as (i) acquisition of a trade secret of another by a person who knows or has reason to know that the trade secret was acquired by improper means; or (ii) disclosure or use of a trade secret of another without expressed or implied consent. The improper means[192] include theft, bribery, misrepresentation, breach or inducement of a breach of a duty to maintain secrecy, or *espionage through electronic or other means.*

The trade secret owner can obtain injunctive relief for actual or threatened misappropriation. In addition to or in lieu of injunctive relief, the owner of the trade secret can ask for monetary relief, which includes actual lost profits, unjust enrichment and reasonable royalty for a misappropriator's unauthorized disclosure or use of a trade secret. If willful and malicious misappropriation exists, the court may award exemplary damages.

A court shall preserve the secrecy of alleged trade secrets by reasonable means, which may include granting protective orders in connection with discovery proceedings, holding in-camera hearings, sealing the records of the action and ordering any person involved in the litigation not to disclose alleged trade secrets without prior court approval.

---

191 US Chamber of Commerce, The Case for Enhanced Protection of Trade Secrets in the Trans-Pacific Partnership Agreement (2013) 23.

192 Improper means could include otherwise lawful conduct which is improper under the circumstances, e.g., an airplane overflight used as aerial reconnaissance to determine the competitor's plant layout during construction of the plant. *E. I. du Pont de Nemours & Co., Inc.* v. *Christopher*, 431 F.2d 1012 (CA5, 1970), cert. den. 400 US 1024 (1970). Because the trade secret can be destroyed through public knowledge, the unauthorized disclosure of a trade secret is also a misappropriation.

Computer fraud

Another domestic legal tool to combat cyberespionage under the American legal system is the Computer Fraud and Abuse Act. According to the act, unauthorized access to a computer and obtaining information is a punishable crime. Title 18, Section 1030 (a) of the United States Code provides that whoever accessed a computer without authorization or exceeding authorized access and thereby obtained information is punishable.[193]

The crime of computer fraud consists of three essential elements. First, the defendant should intentionally access a computer without authorization or by exceeding authorized access. This behavior constitutes the *actus*

---

193 Title 18, Section 1030(a) of the United States Code read as follows:

(a) Whoever –

(1) having knowingly accessed a computer without authorization or exceeding authorized access, and by means of such conduct having obtained information … such information so obtained could be used to the injury of the United States, or to the advantage of any foreign nation willfully communicates, delivers, transmits, or causes to be communicated, delivered, or transmitted, or attempts to communicate, deliver, transmit or cause to be communicated, delivered, or transmitted the same to any person not entitled to receive it, or willfully retains the same and fails to deliver it to the officer or employee of the United States entitled to receive it;

(2) intentionally accesses a computer without authorization or exceeds authorized access, and thereby obtains –

(A) information contained in a financial record of a financial institution, or of a card issuer as defined in section 1602(n) of title 15, or contained in a file of a consumer reporting agency on a consumer, as such terms are defined in the Fair Credit Reporting Act (15 U.S.C. 1681 et seq.);

(B) information from any department or agency of the United States; or

(C) information from any protected computer;

(3) intentionally, without authorization to access any nonpublic computer of a department or agency of the United States, accesses such a computer of that department or agency that is exclusively for the use of the Government of the United States or, in the case of a computer not exclusively for such use, is used by or for the Government of the United States and such conduct affects that use by or for the Government of the United States;

(4) knowingly and with intent to defraud, accesses a protected computer without authorization, or exceeds authorized access, and by means of such conduct furthers the intended fraud and obtains anything of value, unless the object of the fraud and the thing obtained consists only of the use of the computer and the value of such use is not more than $5,000 in any 1-year period;

reus part of the typology of the crime. Second, the defendant should obtain information (1) contained in a financial record of a financial institution or an issuer of a credit card or (2) on a costumer contained in a file of a consumer reporting agency (3) from any department/agency of the United States, or (4) from any protected computer. The defendant should have specific intentions to perpetrate such activities. In other words, one should act (1) for the purposes of commercial advantage or private personal gain (2) in furtherance of the described criminal or tortious act, or (3) obtained information having a value exceeding 5,000.00 US Dollars. In this regard, the above-mentioned *mens rea* element should coexist with the *actus reus* element for crimes to be committed.

Title 18, Section 1030 (a) of the United States Code set out the punishment for the above-mentioned crimes.[194]

---

194 Title 18, Section 1030(a) of the United States Code read as follows:
  (b) Whoever conspires to commit or attempts to commit an offense under subsection (a) of this section shall be punished as provided in subsection (c) of this section.
  (c) The punishment for an offense under subsection (a) or (b) of this section is –
    (1)
    (A) a fine under this title or imprisonment for not more than ten years, or both, in the case of an offense under subsection (a)(1) of this section which does not occur after a conviction for another offense under this section, or an attempt to commit an offense punishable under this subparagraph; and
    (B) a fine under this title or imprisonment for not more than twenty years, or both, in the case of an offense under subsection (a)(1) of this section which occurs after a conviction for another offense under this section, or an attempt to commit an offense punishable under this subparagraph;
    (2)
    (A) except as provided in subparagraph (B), a fine under this title or imprisonment for not more than one year, or both, in the case of an offense under subsection (a) (2), (a) (3), or (a) (6) of this section which does not occur after a conviction for another offense under this section, or an attempt to commit an offense punishable under this subparagraph;
    (B) a fine under this title or imprisonment for not more than 5 years, or both, in the case of an offense under subsection (a)(2), or an attempt to commit an offense punishable under this subparagraph, if –
      (i) the offense was committed for purposes of commercial advantage or private financial gain;
      (ii) the offense was committed in furtherance of any criminal or tortious act in violation of the Constitution or laws of the United States or of any State; or
      (iii) the value of the information obtained exceeds $5,000; and
    (C) a fine under this title or imprisonment for not more than ten years, or both, in the case of an offense under subsection (a)(2), (a)(3) or (a)(6)

Section 1030 (a) (2) does not impose fines. Although there is no "monetary threshold for establishing a misdemeanor offense under section 1030 (a) (2), the value of the information obtained during an intrusion can elevate the crime to a felony."[195] Violations of section 1030 (a) (2) are misdemeanors punishable by a fine or a one-year prison term unless aggravating factors apply. A violation or attempted violation of section 1030 (a) (2) is a felony (otherwise it is a misdemeanor) if: (1) committed for commercial advantage or private financial gain, (2) committed in furtherance of any criminal or tortious act in violation of the Constitution or laws of the United States or of any state, or (3) the value of the information obtained exceeds 5,000 dollars.

Merely obtaining information worth less than 5,000 USD is a misdemeanor unless committed after a conviction for another offense under section 1030, in which case the maximum prison term is 10 years.

Briefly, section 1030 requires that the defendant actually access a computer without or in excess of authorization. Merely viewing information is sufficient to be understood as "obtaining information" even without downloading or copying a file. Department or agency includes any federal government entity, including the legislature, judiciary, and all parts of the Executive Branch. Whether a company working as a private contractor for the government constitutes a "department or agency of the United States" for purposes of prosecution under subsection (a) (2) (B) are intended to be covered by this section.[196] Any reasonable method can be used for fulfilling the requirement to determine the value of the information. For example, the research, development

> of this section which occurs after a conviction for another offense under this section, or an attempt to commit an offense punishable under this subparagraph;
>
> (3)
> (A) a fine under this title or imprisonment for not more than five years, or both, in the case of an offense under subsection (a)(4) or (a)(7) of this section which does not occur after a conviction for another offense under this section, or an attempt to commit an offense punishable under this subparagraph; and
> (B) a fine under this title or imprisonment for not more than ten years, or both, in the case of an offense under subsection (a)(4), or (a)(7) of this section which occurs after a conviction for another offense under this section, or an attempt to commit an offense punishable under this subparagraph.

195 H. Marshall Jarrett and Michael W. Bailie, Prosecuting Computer Crimes, Office of Legal Education Executive Office for United States Attorneys (2015), 17.
196 Ibid.

and manufacturing costs or the value of the property "in the thieves' market" can be used to meet the 5,000 USD valuation.[197]

Until 2008, violation of section 1030 (a) (2) (C) required actual interstate or foreign communication.[198] This limitation precluded prosecution in serious cases where sensitive or proprietary information was stolen from within a single state, as is often the case with "insider" thefts. Through the Identity Theft Enforcement and Restitution Act, Congress deleted the portion of section 1030 (a) (2) (C) that required interstate or foreign communication. Accordingly, the government may now prosecute those who steal information from a computer without regard to how or where the criminal gained access to the victim's computer, so long as that computer constitutes a "protected computer."

Due to the complex and long bureaucratic characteristic of the extradition process or lack of any bilateral agreement, domestic legal actions against criminals or perpetrators outside of the territories of states are preponderantly ineffective. Even if states signed a mutual legal assistance agreement,[199] the success of domestic criminal actions are low. However, as a part of the naming and shaming campaign, which is a political action, governments apply to courts for obtaining arrest warrants or bringing a criminal case against perpetrators. For instance, in order to confront Chinese economic and industrial espionage activities, a grand jury in the western district of Pennsylvania indicted five Chinese military hackers for economic espionage against the US nuclear power, metals and solar products industries for commercial advantage.[200] The US Department of Justice's indictment of these hackers was actually a domestic response, but also politically a part of the naming and shaming campaign against China's economic and industrial espionage activities.[201]

To conclude, domestic legal systems offer several provisions enabling ways to combat cyberespionage. However, these provisions target

197 Title 18 U.S.C., Section 1831 Economic Espionage.
198 See 18 U.S.C. § 1030(a) (2)(C) (2007).
199 Agreement on Mutual Legal Assistance in Criminal Matters, US-China (19 June 2000) www.state.gov/documents/organization/126977.pdf (accessed 25 June 2015).
200 US Department of Justice, "US Charges Five Chinese Military Hackers with Cyber Espionage Against US Corporations and a Labor Organization for Commercial Advantage" (19 May 2014) www.fbi.gov/pittsburgh/press-releases/2014/u.s.-charges-five-chinese-military-hackers-with-cyber-espionage-against-u.s.-corporations-and-a-labor-organization-for-commercial-advantage (accessed 25 June 2015).
201 Scott J. Shackelford, *Managing Cyber Attacks in International Law, Business, and Relations in Search of Cyber Peace*, Cambridge: Cambridge University Press (2014), 11.

individuals or organizations who are responsible for cyberespionage activities. The next chapter will cover appropriate legal responses under international law and provisions applicable to states rather than individuals and organizations.

European regulations

European trade secret protection

The EU and its member states are signatories to the WTO Agreement including the TRIPS Agreement; therefore, they are obliged to comply with article 39 of the TRIPS Agreement, requiring the adoption of legislation for the protection of trade secrets, and to notify the WTO whenever they issued such protection. Following a proposal of the European Council, on 8 June 2016, the European Parliament and the Council adopted Directive 2016/943 (the Directive)[202] that aims to standardize the national laws in EU countries against the unlawful acquisition, disclosure and use of trade secrets. Contrary to the EU Regulations, directives are not self-executing therefore EU member states should adopt laws that comply with each directive.[203] In this sense, every member state can adopt a protection in accordance with principles enshrined in the Directive.

According to the European Commission, the Directive intended to harmonize "the definition of trade secrets in accordance with existing internationally binding standards. It also defines the relevant forms of misappropriation and clarifies that reverse engineering and parallel innovation must be guaranteed given that trade secrets are not a form of exclusive intellectual property right."[204] There are several underlying reasons for enacting the Directive. According to the Directive, "innovative businesses are increasingly exposed to dishonest practices aimed at misappropriating trade secrets, such as theft, unauthorized copying, *economic espionage* or the breach of confidentiality requirements, whether from within or from outside of the Union."[205]

---

202 European Parliament and The Council, Directive 2016/943, "On the Protection of Undisclosed Know-How and Business Information (Trade Secrets) Against Their Unlawful Acquisition, Use and Disclosure" (8 June 2016).
203 Paul Craig and Gráinne de Búrca, *EU Law: Text, Cases and Materials*, 6th edn, Oxford: Oxford University Press (2015), 108.
204 European Commission, Trade Secrets, https://ec.europa.eu/growth/industry/intellectual-property/trade-secrets_en (accessed 4 June 2018).
205 Directive 2016/943, para. (4).

Considering *economic espionage*, the European Union has significant experience, which paves the way for taking necessary precautions against economic cyberespionage. In 2000, a report published by the European Parliament claimed and argued that the US was using the communications interception system, known as ECHELON, to intercept European businesses and passing on the "competitive intelligence" collected through this system to US firms.[206] The report states that the gathering of economic data, such as details of developments in individual sectors of the economy, trends on commodity markets, compliance with economic embargoes, observance of rules on supplying dual-use goods, etc., is a part of the remit of foreign intelligence services and firms are often subject to surveillance.[207]
Furthermore, according to the report,

> the U.S. intelligence services do not merely investigate general economic facts but also intercept detailed communications between firms, particularly where contracts are being awarded, and they justify this on the grounds of combating attempted bribery. Therefore, detailed interception poses the risk that information may be used for the purpose of competitive intelligence-gathering rather than combating corruption, even though the U.S. and the United Kingdom state that they do not do so.[208]

The report also asserts, "authoritative sources confirmed the US Congress Brown Report, indicating that 5 percent of intelligence gathered via non-open sources is used as economic intelligence; whereas it was assumed by the same sources that this intelligence surveillance could enable the US industry to earn up to 7 billion USD in contracts."[209] In addition to that, the report underlined that:

> the situation becomes intolerable when intelligence services allow themselves to be used for the purposes of gathering competitive intelligence by spying on foreign firms with the aim of securing a competitive advantage for firms in the home country, and whereas it is frequently maintained that the global interception system has been used in this way, although no such case has been substantiated,

206 EU Parliament, Report on the Existence of A Global System for the Interception of Private and Commercial Communications (ECHELON interception system) (2001/2098(INI)).
207 Ibid., para. (O), 13.
208 Ibid., para. (P), 13.
209 Ibid., para. (S), 14.

Whereas sensitive commercial data are principally kept inside individual firms, so that competitive intelligence-gathering in particular involves efforts to obtain information through members of staff or through people planted in the firm for this purpose or else, more and more commonly, by hacking into internal computer networks;

Whereas risk and security awareness in small and medium-sized firms is often inadequate and the dangers of economic espionage and the interception of communications are not recognized.[210]

The report concluded its findings that

if an ECHELON type system is used purely for intelligence purposes, there is no violation of EU law, since operations in the interests of state security are not subject to the EC Treaty, but would fall under Title V of the Treaty on European Union (CFSP). However, if such a system is misused for the purposes of gathering competitive intelligence, such action is at odds with the Member States' duty of loyalty and with the concept of a common market based on free competition, so that a Member State participating in such a system violates EC law.[211]

Several recommendations are proposed to ensure effective protection regarding: 1) the amendment of international agreements on the protection of citizens and firms, 2) national legislative measures to protect citizens and firms, 3) specific legal measures to combat industrial espionage, 4) measures concerning the implementation of the law and the monitoring of that implementation, 5) measures to encourage self-protection by citizens and firms, and 6) measures to improve security in the institutions and other measures. Under the specific legal measures to combat industrial espionage, the report addressed the member states:

The Member States are called upon to consider to what extent industrial espionage and the payment of bribes as a way of securing contracts can be combated by means of European and international legal provisions and, especially, whether WTO rules could be adopted which take account of the distortions of competition brought about by such practices, for example by rendering

---

contracts obtained in this way null and void. The USA, Canada, Australia and New Zealand are called upon to participate this initiative.

The Member States are called upon to give a binding undertaking neither to engage in industrial espionage, either directly or behind the front offered by a foreign power active on their territory, nor to allow a foreign power to carry out such espionage from their territory, thereby acting in accordance with the letter and spirit of the EC Treaty.

The Member States and the U.S. Administration are called upon to start an open U.S.-EU dialogue on economic intelligence-gathering.

The Member States are called upon to ensure that their intelligence services are not misused for the purposes of obtaining competitive intelligence, since this would be at odds with the Member States' duty of loyalty and the concept of a common market based on free competition.[212]

According to article 2 of the Directive, trade secret means "information which meets all of the following requirements:

(a) it is secret in the sense that it is not, as a body or in the precise configuration and assembly of its components, generally known among or readily accessible to persons within the circles that normally deal with the kind of information in question;

(b) it has commercial value because it is secret;

(c) it has been subject to reasonable steps under the circumstances, by the person lawfully in control of the information, to keep it secret."[213]

Without establishing criminal sanctions, harmonizing the civil means through which victims of trade secret misappropriation can seek protection are by: (a) stopping the unlawful use and further disclosure of misappropriated trade secrets, (b) the removal from the market of goods that have been manufactured on the basis of a trade secret that has been illegally acquired, or (c) the right to compensation for the damages caused by the unlawful use or disclosure of the misappropriated trade secret.

According to article 10, member states shall ensure that the competent judicial authorities may, at the request of the trade secret holder,

212 Ibid.
213 Directive 2016/943, Art. 2.

order any of the following provisional and precautionary measures against the alleged infringer:

(a) the cessation of or, as the case may be, the prohibition of the use or disclosure of the trade secret on a provisional basis;
(b) the prohibition of the production, offering, placing on the market or use of infringing goods, or the importation, export or storage of infringing goods for those purposes;
(c) the seizure or delivery up of the suspected infringing goods, including imported goods, so as to prevent their entry into, or circulation on, the market.[214]

Pursuant to article 14 of the Directive, member states shall ensure that the competent judicial authorities, upon the request of the injured party, order an infringer who knew or ought to have known that he, she or it was engaging in unlawful acquisition, use or disclosure of a trade secret, to pay the trade secret holder damages appropriate to the actual prejudice suffered as a result of the unlawful acquisition, use or disclosure of the trade secret.[215]

To this end, after the ECHELON incident, there was not any progress to restrict industrial espionage activities. However, it was publicly announced that there should be a limit setting rule, regulations, and administrative procedures on industrial espionage activities. The Directive on the protection of trade secrets is an outcome of such a campaign; supporting the production of an international norm that industrial espionage is not acceptable. Within the framework of the Directive Article 4(2–3), we can identify two types of cybercrime offenses stipulated under the European Convention on Cybercrime and the EU Directive 2013/40, namely, illegal access and illegal interception. These offenses fulfill the conditions of (i) intentionally (ii) unauthorized access to information (iii) held on electronic files.[216]

European cybercrime protection

The Cybersecurity Strategy of the European Union,[217] published in 2013, states that cyberspace should be protected from incidents,

214 Directive 2016/943, art. 10.
215 Directive 2016/943, art. 14.
216 Marco Alexandre Saias, "Unlawful acquisition of trade secrets by cyber theft: between the proposed directive on trade secrets and the directive on cyber attacks," *JIPLP*, 9(9) (2015), 724.
217 European Commission, Cybersecurity Strategy of the European Union: An Open, Safe and Secure Cyberspace, 52013JC0001 (2013).

malicious activities and misuse; and governments have a significant role in ensuring a free and safe cyberspace. The EU economy is already affected by cyber crime[218] activities against the private sector and individuals. According to the document, "cyber criminals are using ever more sophisticated methods for intruding into information systems, stealing critical data or holding companies to ransom. The increase of economic espionage and state-sponsored activities in cyberspace poses a new category of threats for EU governments and companies."[219] The document underlined that the EU does not call for the creation of new international legal instruments for cyber issues.[220]

Within the document, there are references to cyberespionage with regard to EU support in case of a major cyber incident or attack. Pursuant to the document:

If the incident seems to relate to cyber espionage or a state-sponsored attack, or has national security implications, national security and defense authorities will alert their relevant counterparts, so that they know they are under attack and can defend themselves. Early warning mechanisms will then be activated and, if required, so will crisis management or other procedures. A particularly serious cyber incident or attack could constitute sufficient ground for a Member State to invoke the EU Solidarity Clause (Article 222 of the Treaty on the Functioning of the European Union).[221]

218 This definition is accepted by the Cybersecurity Strategy document of the EU: cybercrime commonly refers to a broad range of different criminal activities where computers and information systems are involved either as a primary tool or as a primary target. Cybercrime comprises traditional offenses (e.g. fraud, forgery and identity theft), content-related offenses (e.g. online distribution of child pornography or incitement to racial hatred) and offenses unique to computers and information systems (e.g. attacks against information systems, denial of service and malware).
219 European Commission, Cybersecurity Strategy (2013).
220 Ibid.: "To address cybercrime, the Budapest Convention is an instrument open for adoption by third countries. It provides a model for drafting national cybercrime legislation and a basis for international co-operation in this field. If armed conflicts extend to cyberspace, International Humanitarian Law and, as appropriate, Human Rights law will apply to the case at hand."
221 According to the Article 222 of the Treaty on the Functioning of the European Union:
   1. The Union and its Member States shall act jointly in a spirit of solidarity if a Member State is the object of a terrorist attack or the victim of a natural or man-made disaster. The Union shall mobilize all the instruments at its disposal, including the military resources made available by the Member States, to:

The European Convention on Cybercrime[222] (the Convention) and the EU Directive 2013/40 on Attacks against Information Systems are key significant legal documents at the EU level, and they aim to tackle cyber attacks and foster cooperation between signatory states.

EUROPEAN CONVENTION ON CYBERCRIME

Signed in 2001, The Convention is the first binding international legal document regulating cybercrimes especially, infringement of copyrights, computer-related fraud, child pornography, hate crimes and violations of network security.[223] Forty-nine states have ratified the Convention from the date the treaty opened for signature.[224] The purpose of the Convention is enshrined in the preamble as:

> (a) prevent the terrorist threat in the territory of the Member States;
> - protect democratic institutions and the civilian population from any terrorist attack;
> - assist a Member State in its territory, at the request of its political authorities, in the event of a terrorist attack;
> (b) assist a Member State in its territory, at the request of its political authorities, in the event of a natural or man-made disaster.
> 2. Should a Member State be the object of a terrorist attack or the victim of a natural or man-made disaster, the other Member States shall assist it at the request of its political authorities. To that end, the Member States shall coordinate between themselves in the Council.

222 Council of Europe, Convention on Cybercrime, European Treaty Series – No. 185 (signed 23 November 2001, in effect 1 July 2004): "it is also called Budapest Convention on Cybercrime or the Budapest Convention." Turkey signed the Convention on 10 November 2010 and ratified 22 April 2014.

223 Views on legal nature of the Convention see: Marco Gercke, "Understanding cybercrime: phenomena, challenges and legal response", Geneva: International Telecommunication Union (2012) www.itu.int/ITU-D/cyb/cybersecurity/legislation.html; Michael Vatis, "The Council of Europe's Convention on Cybercrime," in *Proceedings of a Workshop on Deterring CyberAttacks: Informing Strategies and Developing Options for US Policy* Washington, DC: National Academic Press (2010), 207, 212; Amalie Weber, "The Council of Europe Convention on Cybercrime," *Berkeley Technology Law Journal*, 18 (2014), 441; Mike Keyser, "The Council of Europe Convention on Cybercrime," *Journal of Transnational Law and Policy*, 12 (2003), 287; Shannon Hopkins, "Cybercrime convention: a positive beginning to a long road ahead," *Journal of High Technology Law*, 2 (2003), 107.

224 Nine of them are non-member States of Council of Europe (Australia, Canada, Dominican Republic, Israel, Japan, Mauritius, Panama, Sri Lanka, United States of America), see other states http://conventions.coe.int/Treaty/Commun/ChercheSig.asp?NT=185&CM=1&DF=20/02/2015&CL=ENG (accessed 4 June 2018).

Convention is necessary to deter action directed against the confidentiality, integrity and availability of computer systems, networks and computer data as well as the misuse of such systems, networks and data by providing for the criminalization of such conduct, as described in this Convention, and the adoption of powers sufficient for effectively combating such criminal offenses, by facilitating their detection, investigation and prosecution at both the domestic and international levels and by providing arrangements for fast and reliable international cooperation.

In this regard, the Convention stipulates cyber crimes which can be adopted against cyberespionage, namely, (1) offenses against the confidentiality, integrity, and availability of computer data and systems and (2) computer-related offenses. Article 2 of the Convention regulates illegal access; in other words, unauthorized access to the whole or any part of a computer system. This offense should be committed intentionally. Moreover, the article envisaged that the offense could be committed by infringing security measures, with the intent of obtaining computer data or other dishonest intent, or in relation to a computer system that is connected to another computer system.

Article 3 of the Convention regulates illegal interception, which covers APT-type attacks. The Convention criminalizes the interception without right, made by technical means, of non-public transmissions of computer data to, from or within a computer system, including electromagnetic emissions from a computer system carrying such computer data. This crime should be committed intentionally. Similar to article 2, this offense can be committed with dishonest intent, or in relation to a computer system that is connected to another computer system.

Articles 4 and 5 of the Convention regulate the data and system interference. Pursuant to article 4, data interference offense is committed by damaging, deletion, deterioration, alteration or suppression of computer data without right. This offense again should be committed intentionally. With regard to article 5, system interference is committed by serious hindering without right of the functioning of a computer system by inputting, transmitting, damaging, deleting, deteriorating, altering or suppressing computer data.

Like the articles of the Wassenaar Arrangement regulating and restricting trade of intrusion and surveillance items, the Convention regulates the misuse of devices under article 6. Pursuant to the article, it is seen as a criminal offense when committed intentionally and without right a) the production, sale, procurement for use, import, distribution or otherwise making available of i) a device, including a computer program, designed or adapted primarily for the purpose of committing any of the offenses established in accordance with Articles 2 through 5; ii) a computer password, access code or similar data by which the whole or any part of a computer system is capable of being accessed, with intent that it be used for the purpose of committing any of the offenses established in Articles 2 through 5; and b) the possession of an item referred to in paragraphs i) or ii) above, with intent that it be used for the purpose of committing any of the offenses established in Articles 2 through 5.

Computer-related offenses; especially computer-related forgery and fraud are regulated under Articles 7 and 8 of the Convention. Computer-related fraud is relevant to cyberespionage. Article 8 establishes a criminal offense when committed intentionally and without right, the causing of a loss of property to another person by (1) any input, alteration, deletion or suppression of computer data and (2) any interference with the functioning of a computer system with fraudulent or dishonest intent of procuring, without right, an economic benefit for oneself or for another person. Therefore, "causing of a loss of property," "procuring, without right, an economic benefit" are economic and industrial cyberespionage activities.

DIRECTIVE 2013/40 ON ATTACKS AGAINST INFORMATION SYSTEMS

The Cybercrime Convention is the legal framework of reference for combating cybercrime, including attacks against information systems. This Directive[225] builds on that Convention. This Directive aims to amend and expand the provisions of the Council Framework Decision.[226]

The objectives of the Directive 2016/943 are explained as: 1) to approximate the criminal law of the member states in the area of attacks against information systems by establishing minimum rules concerning the definition of criminal offenses and the relevant sanctions and 2) to improve cooperation between competent authorities, including the police and other specialized law enforcement services of the member states, as well as the competent specialized EU agencies and bodies, such as Eurojust, Europol and its European Cyber Crime Center, and the European Network and Information Security Agency (ENISA). Common definitions and approaches to the constituent elements of

---

225 European Parliament and The Council, Directive 2013/40, "On Attacks Against Information Systems and Replacing Council Framework Decision 2005/222/JHA," *Official Journal of European Union* L218/8 (2013).
226 Council Framework Decision, 2005/222/JHA of 24 February 2005 on attacks against information systems.

criminal offenses, such as illegal access to an information system, illegal system interference, illegal data interference and illegal interception aim to ensure this approximation.

In the preamble, the Directive 2016/943 underlined that "large-scale cyber attacks can cause substantial economic damage both through the interruption of information systems and communication and through the loss or alteration of commercially important confidential information or other data."[227] Article 1 of the Directive 2013/40 states that the Directive establishes minimum rules concerning the definition of criminal violations and sanctions in the area of attacks against information systems. It also aims to facilitate the prevention of such violations and to improve cooperation between judicial and other competent authorities.[228] In addition, Article 9 underlined that the offenses referred to in Articles 3 to 8 are punishable by effective, proportionate and dissuasive criminal penalties. Therefore, the Directive determines the minimum limit of punishment for offenses stipulated under Articles 3 to 8.

Contrary to the Convention, the Directive defines the term "without right" as a conduct referred to in this Directive, including access, interference or interception, which is not authorized by the owner or by another right holder of the system or of part of it, or not permitted under national law.[229]

Pursuant to article 3, illegal access to information systems is criminalized when committed intentionally or accessed without right, to the whole or to any part of an information system, and is punishable as a criminal offense when committed by infringing a security measure, at least for cases which are not minor.[230]

Articles 4 and 5, which are almost identical to articles 4 and 5 of the Convention, criminalized illegal system and data interference. Pursuant to article 4, seriously hindering or interrupting the functioning of an information system by inputting computer data, by transmitting, damaging, deleting, deteriorating, altering or suppressing such data, or by rendering such data inaccessible, intentionally and without right, is punishable as a criminal offense.[231] According to article 5, deleting, damaging, deteriorating, altering or suppressing computer data on an information system, or rendering such data inaccessible, intentionally

---

227 European Parliament and The Council, Directive 2013/40, "On Attacks Against Information Systems," para. (6).
228 Ibid., art. 1.
229 Ibid., art. 2.
230 Ibid., art. 3.
231 Ibid., art. 4.

and without right, is punishable as a criminal offense.[232] Offenses referred to in articles 4 and 5, when committed intentionally, are punishable by a maximum term of imprisonment of at least three years when a significant amount of information systems have been affected through the use of a tool, referred to in article 7, designed or adapted primarily for that purpose. Offenses referred to in articles 4 and 5 are punishable by a maximum term of imprisonment of at least five years if:

(a) they are committed within the framework of a criminal organization, as defined in Framework Decision 2008/841/JHA, irrespective of the penalty provided for therein;
(b) they cause serious damage; or
(c) they are committed against a critical infrastructure information system.

Article 6 relates to illegal interception. Although it is not defined under the article, interception is defined under the preamble. Accordingly, the preamble states that interception includes, but is not necessarily limited to, the listening to, monitoring or surveillance of the content of communications and the procuring of the content of data either directly through access and use of the information systems, or indirectly through the use of electronic eavesdropping or tapping devices by technical means.[233] Furthermore, pursuant to article 6, intercepting, by technical means, non-public transmissions of computer data to, from or within an information system, including electromagnetic emissions from an information system carrying such computer data, intentionally and without right, is punishable as a criminal offense.[234]

Article 7 focuses on the tools used for committing offenses. Accordingly, the intentional production, sale, procurement for use, import, distribution or otherwise making available of one of the following tools, without right and with the intention that it be used to commit any of the offenses referred to in articles 3 to 6, is punishable as a criminal offense at least for cases which are not minor:

(a) a computer program, designed or adapted primarily for the purpose of committing any of the offenses referred to in Articles 3 to 6;
(b) a computer password, access code, or similar data by which the whole or any part of an information system is capable of being accessed.

---

232 Ibid., art. 5.
233 Ibid., para. (9).
234 Ibid., art. 6.

According to article 9, offenses referred to in articles 3, 6, 7 and 8 are punishable by a maximum term of imprisonment of at least two years. More importantly, the Directive regulates the liability of and sanctions against legal persons. Pursuant to article 10, legal persons can be held liable for offenses referred to in articles 3 to 8, committed for their benefit by any person, acting either individually or as part of a body of the legal person, and having a leading position within the legal person, based on one of the following:

(a) a power of representation of the legal person;
(b) an authority to take decisions on behalf of the legal person;
(c) an authority to exercise control within the legal person.[235]

Regarding sanctions against legal persons, article 11 states that a legal person held liable pursuant to article 10(1) is punishable by effective, proportionate and dissuasive sanctions, which shall include criminal or non-criminal fines and which may include other sanctions, such as:

(a) exclusion from entitlement to public benefits or aid;
(b) temporary or permanent disqualification from the practice;
    of commercial activities;
(c) placing under judicial supervision;
(d) judicial winding up;
(e) temporary or permanent closure of establishments which have been used for committing the offense.[236]

In light of the above explanations, we concluded that continental legal systems have adopted an approach to tackle economic and industrial cyberespionage through regulating cyber crimes criminalizing unauthorized access to trade secrets. However, the common law system has proposed and adopted *lex specialis* dealing only with economic and industrial cyberespionage. In this regard, the common law system offers heavy fines and imprisonment for actors of such operations.

Conclusion

The world has experienced a revolution in information technologies, which significantly influence various aspects of society. First, it became easier to generate, transmit and store data. Second, the cost of

235 Ibid., art. 10.
236 Ibid., art. 11.

Table 2.1 Comparison of traditional espionage and cyberespionage

	Traditional espionage	Cyberespionage
Target	• Political intelligence • Military intelligence • New weapons systems, military strategies or information about the stationing of troops	• High-tech products • Commercial enterprises • IT, genetics, aviation, lasers, optics, electronics
Purpose	To gain: • Political supremacy • Military supremacy • Tactical supremacy	To gain: • Commercial advantage, • Upper hand in negotiations • Technological advantage
Means/Tools	• Human-based intelligence • Field operations	• Communication or signal-based intelligence • Cyber weapons: APT
Actors	• States	• States • Corporations • Criminal organizations • Hackers

collecting, storing and transmitting data sharply decreased. Therefore, interactions and relations between society and its environment became dependent on technological devices.

Furthermore, espionage has also undergone a transformation due to developments experienced in information technologies. The understanding of war has shifted from total war to hybrid war, including cyber activities, insurgencies and economic warfare. Additionally, purpose and targets, methods and means, actors and incidents of espionage have been altered as illustrated in Table 2.1.

Espionage activities have shifted from human-based intelligence to technology-based intelligence; from times of peace to times of war. The mass collection of data, dragnet applications, cyberespionage and infiltration became easily accessible tools not only for states but also for criminal organizations, hackers, etc. Although such activities have legally grounded preventive measures, the national security of states, their targets, purposes, tools and actors of espionage has altered. In addition to the change observed in features of espionage activities, more importantly, they have begun to be deployed frequently in peacetime rather than wartime.

International legal approaches to espionage activities underline that peacetime espionage activities are not prohibited by international law.

Table 2.2 Regulation of wartime cyber/espionage

Time	Type	Level	Regulation
Wartime	Espionage	Domestic	Prohibited / regulated
		International	Allowed / regulated
	Cyberespionage	Domestic	Prohibited/ partly regulated
		International	Allowed /partly regulated

Table 2.3 Regulation of peacetime cyber/espionage

Time	Type	Level	Regulation
Peacetime	Espionage	Domestic	Prohibited / regulated
		International	Allowed / not regulated
	Cyberespionage	Domestic	Prohibited / regulated
		International	Allowed / partly regulated

What is not prohibited is allowed, as per the *Lotus* case. However, wartime espionage activities are allowed under international law and there is vast literature about state practices.

Peacetime espionage and cyberespionage activities can be penalized under domestic laws. Targets can be trade secrets and assets protected under regulations relating to intellectual property and protection of trade secrets. Additionally, cyberespionage activities are criminalized under cyber crimes such as unauthorized access and illegal interception. With regard to cyberespionage activities where they aim to gain commercial advantage or the upper hand in negotiations, they are also subject to certain sanctions, as a violation of principles such as good faith, fair trade, fair and free negotiations, and economic sovereignty.

Peacetime cyberespionage activities are not prohibited explicitly by any international legal document. Therefore, it is acknowledged that these activities are allowed under international law. As we have discussed, due to the special nature of economic and industrial cyberespionage, they can provide a basis for state responsibility with regard to violation of several principles of customary international law. In this, legal options such as countermeasures or retorsion can be adopted. With regard to their targets as high-tech products and trade secrets, such activities are prohibited by the TRIPS Agreement and states are obliged to take necessary legal measures to provide protection for such values. There is also an international obligation that member states of the WTO should fulfill. Allowing any of its subjects to conduct cyberespionage provides that legal protections in the state in question are not sufficient to fulfill WTO obligations.

What is next?

International research firm Gartner estimates that there will be approximately 20 billion Internet-connected devices consisting not only of smartphones and computers but also of wearable, smart home devices or smarter products and machine-to-machine devices in 2020.[237] Therefore, along with human-generated data we will have machine-generated data as well. At this point, companies or governments need the ability to analyze, find and identify patterns and need to separate the redundant data. The recent advancement in Artificial Intelligence (AI) will certainly ease this process.

Moreover, it is estimated that AI application of warfare and espionage and military use of AI is inevitable.[238] The application of AI to espionage will not augment only the power and ability to collect data but also effectively analyze big data polls. This will also make the attacks more sophisticated and undetectable. Intelligence agencies have begun to invest in AI and its application to espionage operations. To illustrate, the National Geospatial-Intelligence Agency, who collect, analyze and interpret images beamed from drones, satellites and other feeds around the globe, e.g. military testing sites, has announced its investment in AI to automate the process.[239] Likewise, the CIA recently has "137 different artificial intelligence pilot projects underway."[240]

AI researches have already ignited a new global arms race in the technology domain.[241] Brzezinski outlined the reason for the US victory

237 Mark Hung (ed.), "Leading the IoT," Gartner (2017), 2.
238 Greg Allen and Taniel Chan, "Artificial intelligence and national security," Belfer Center Study (July 2017), 50: "Advances in artificial intelligence, and a subset called machine learning are occurring much faster than expected and will provide US military and intelligence services with powerful new high-technology warfare and spying capabilities. AI will dramatically augment autonomous weapons and espionage capabilities and will represent a key aspect of future military power."
239 Jenna Mclaughlin, "Artificial intelligence will put spies out of work, too," *Foreign Policy* (9 June 2017) http://foreignpolicy.com/2017/06/09/artificial-intelligence-will-put-spies-out-of-work-too/ (accessed 10 January 2018).
240 Jenna Mclaughlin, "The robots will run the CIA, too," *Foreign Policy*, 7 (September 2017) http://foreignpolicy.com/2017/09/07/the-robots-will-run-the-cia-too/ (accessed 10 January 2018).
241 Tom Simonite, "For superpowers, artificial intelligence fuels new global arms race," Wired (9 August 2017) www.wired.com/story/for-superpowers-artificial-intelligence-fuels-new-global-arms-race/ (accessed 10 January 2018).

over and the supremacy against the Soviet Union is due to the economic and technological dynamism of the US[242] Today, the technological dynamism the US has enjoyed since the end of Cold War is challenged by China.[243] China has declared in its national AI Strategy Plan[244] that it will lead the world in AI technology and research by 2025. Moreover, "China's strategy recognizes the essential dual-use nature of artificial intelligence. The same core technological capabilities that enable commercial innovation are equally useful for warfare and espionage."[245]

With the AI-enabled cyber attacks and cyber espionage operations, it will be much harder to protect personal data, trade secrets or confidential information. The scale and effect of the attacks will grow exponentially. In this regard, regulating AI and its application will play a significant role. Akin to the creation of treaties, banning chemical and biological weapons or treaties banning nuclear weapons means we should expect to see international treaties, which restrict the military use of AI, hopefully before it is used in a war.

242 Zbigniew Brzezinski, *The Grand Chessboard: American Primacy and Its Geostrategic Imperatives*, New York: Basic Books (2016), 6: "America was simply much richer, technologically much more advanced, militarily more resilient and innovative, socially more creative and appealing."

243 CNAS, Artificial Intelligence and Global Security Summit, Keynote speech given by Eric Schmidt, www.cnas.org/publications/transcript/eric-schmidt-keynote-address-at-the-center-for-a-new-american-security-artificial-intelligence-and-global-security-summit (ccessed 4 June 2018).

244 Graham Webster, Rogier Creemers, Paul Triolo and Elsa Kania, "China's plan to 'lead' in AI: purpose, prospects, and problems," New America (1 August 2017) www.newamerica.org/cybersecurity-initiative/blog/chinas-plan-lead-ai-purpose-prospects-and-problems/ (accessed 10 January 2018).

245 Gregory C. Allen, "China's artificial intelligence strategy poses a credible threat to US tech leadership," Washington, DC: Council on Foreign Relations (4 December 2017) www.cfr.org/blog/chinas-artificial-intelligence-strategy-poses-credible-threat-us-tech-leadership (accessed 10 January 2018).

Bibliography

Aktekin, Uğur and Deniz Doğan Alkan, "Trade secret protection Turkey chapter," in Trevor Cook (ed.), *Trade Secret Protection: A Global Guide*, London: Globe Law and Business (2016).

Alexander, David, "Theft of F-35 design data is helping U.S. adversaries – Pentagon," Reuters (19 June 2013).

Allen, Greg and Taniel Chan, "Artificial intelligence and national security," Harvard: Belfer Center Study (2017).

Allen, Gregory C., "China's artificial intelligence strategy poses a credible threat to U.S. tech leadership," Washington, DC: Council on Foreign Relations (2017).

Anton, Donald K., "The Timor sea treaty arbitration: Timor-Leste challenges Australian espionage and seizure of documents," *ASIL*, 18(6) (2014).

Anton, Donald K., "Arbitrating the treaty on certain maritime arrangements in the Timor Sea," ANU College of Law Research Paper No. 13–20 (2013).

Arangio-Ruiz, Gaetano, *Third Report on State Responsibility*, A/CN.4/440 Yearbook of International Law Commission, Vol. II (1) (1991) para. 24–25 http://legal.un.org/ilc/documentation/english/a_cn4_440.pdf (accessed 4 June 2018).

Arquilla, John, "Cyberwar is already upon us," *Foreign Policy*, 27 February 2012 www.foreignpolicy.com/articles/2012/02/27/cyberwar_is_already_upon_us (accessed 4 June 2018).

Arreguín-Toft, Ivan, *How the Weak Win Wars, A Theory of Asymmetric Conflict*, Cambridge: Cambridge University Press (2005).

Aust, Anthony, *Modern Treaty Law and Practice*, Cambridge: Cambridge University Press (2013).

Barlow, John Perry, "A declaration of the independence of cyberspace," California: Electronic Frontier Foundation (1996).

Bernhardt, Rudolf, *Encyclopedia of International Law* Vol. 4 Amsterdam: North Holland Publishing (1982).

Bin, Cheng, *General Principles of Law as Applied by International Courts and Tribunals*, Cambridge: Cambridge University Press (1953).

Bodansky, Daniel, "Non-Liquet," *Max Planck Encyclopedia of Public International Law* (2006) http://opil.ouplaw.com/view/10.1093/law:epil/9780199231690/law-9780199231690-e1669?prd=EPIL.

Boon, Kristen and Douglas Lovelace, *Terrorism: Commentary on Security Documents Volume 133. The Drone Wars of the 21st Century: Costs and Benefits*, Oxford: Oxford University Press (2014).

Brooks, Rosa, *How Everything Became War and the Military Became Everything*, New York: Simon & Schuster (2016).

Brown, Davis, "A proposal for an international convention to regulate the use of information systems in armed conflict," *HILJ*, 47 (2006).

Brownlie, Ian, *International Law and the Use of Force by States*, Oxford: Clarendon (1963).

Brzezinski, Zbigniew, *The Grand Chessboard: American Primacy and Its Geostrategic Imperatives*, New York: Basic Books (2016).

Buchan, Russell, "Cyberattacks: unlawful uses of force or prohibited interventions?" *Journal of Conflict and Security Law*, 17 (2012), 212–27.

Cassese, Antonio, *International Law*, Oxford: Oxford University Press (2001).

Castro, Daniel, "How much will PRISM cost the U.S. cloud computing industry?," *Information Technology & Innovation Foundation* (August 2013).

Cate, Fred H., *Privacy in Information Age*, Washington, DC: Brookings Institute Press (1997).

Cavelty, Myriam Dunn, *The Militarisation of Cyberspace: Why Less May Be Better*, Tallinn: NATO CCD COE Publications (2012).

Cavelty, Myriam Dunn, *The Militarisation of Cyber Security as a Source of Global Tension, Strategic Trends Analysis*, Zurich, ETH: Center for Security Studies (2012).

Cha, Ariana Eunjung and Ellen Nakashima, "Google China cyberattack part of vast espionage campaign, experts say," *Washington Post* (14 January 2010).

Chin, Josh, "Cyber sleuth track hacker to China's military," *The Wall Street Journal* (2015).

Clarke, Richard, "A global cyber-crisis waiting to happen," *Washington Post* (2013).

Cohen-Jonathan, Gérard and Robert Kovar, "L'espionnage en temps de paix," *Annuaire français de droit international Année*, 6(1) (1960), 1–65.

Cole, Eric, *Advanced Persistent Threat: Understanding the Danger and How to Protect Your Organization*, Waltham: Elsevier (2013).

Colvin, Mark, "Lawyer representing E. Timor alleges ASIO agents raided his practice," *ABC* (2013).

Commentaries on the Draft Articles on Responsibility of States for Internationally Wrongful Acts, Yearbook of International Law Commission, Vol. II (2) (2001), 128.

Cooper, Tim and Ryan LaSalle, *Guarding and Growing Personal Data Value*, London: Accentura (2014).

Craig, Paul and Gráinne de Búrca, *EU Law: Text, Cases and Materials*, 6th Edition, Oxford: Oxford University Press (2015).

D'Amato, Anthony, "Good Faith," in Rudolf Bernhardt (ed.), *Encyclopedia of Public International Law*, 7, Amsterdam: North Holland Publishing (1992), 108–09.

Deeks, Ashley, "An international legal framework for surveillance," *Virginia Journal of International Law*, 55(2) (2015).

Deibert, Ron and Rafal Rohozinski, "Tracking GhostNet: investigating a cyber espionage network," University of Toronto, Munk Centre for International Studies at Trinity College (2009).

Demarest, Geoffrey B., "Espionage in International Law," *DJILP*, 24 (1996), 65–86.

Denning, Dorothy E. and Peter F. MacDoran, "Grounding cyberspace in the physical world," in Alan D. Campen, Douglas H. Dearth and R. Thomas Goodden (eds.), *Cyberwar: Security, Strategy and Coflict in the Information Age*, Fairfax: AFCEA International Press (1996).

Dessemontet, Francois, "Arbitration and confidentiality," *American Review of International Arbitration*, 7 (1996), 300–40.

Dinniss, Heather Harrison, *Cyber Warfare and the Laws of War*, Cambridge: Cambridge University Press (2012).

Dinstein, Yoram, "The principle of distinction and cyber war in international armed conflicts," *Journal of Conflict and Security Law*, 17(2) (2012), 261–77.

Dinstein, Yoram, "Cyber war and international law: concluding remarks at the 2012 Naval War College International Law Conference," *International Law Studies*, 89 (2013), 276–87.

Dinstein, Yoram, "Computer network attacks and self-defense," *International Law Studies*, 76 (2002), 99–119.

Dinstein, Yoram, *War, Aggression and Self Defense*, Cambridge: Cambridge University Press 5th ed. (2011).

Dörr, Oliver and Kirsten Schmalenbach, *Vienna Convention on the Law of Treaties: A Commentary*, Berlin: Springer (2012).

Doyle, Charles, *Stealing Trade Secrets and Economic Espionage: An Overview of 18 U.S.C. 1831 and 1832*, Washington, DC: Congressional Research Service (2014).

Dreyfuss, Rochelle C. and Katherine J. Strandburg (eds), *The Law and Theory of Trade Secrecy: A Handbook of Contemporary Research*, Cheltenham: Edgar Elgar Publishing (2011).

Drummond, David, "A new approach to China," Google Blog (12 January 2010).

Dülger, Murat Volkan, *Bilişim Suçları ve Internet İletişim Hukuku*, İstanbul: Seçkin (2012).

Dwoskin, Elizabeth, "New report: Snowden revelations hurt US companies," Wall Street Journal Digits Blog (2014).

Elias, Olufemi, "The nature of the subjective element in customary international law," *ICLQ*, 44 (1995), 501–20.

EU Parliament, Report on the Existence of A Global System for the Interception of Private and Commercial Communications (ECHELON interception system) (2001/2098(INI)).

Falk, Richard, "Forward," in Roland J. Stanger (ed.), *Essays on Espionage and International Law*, Columbus: Ohio State University Press (1962).

Federal Ministry of Interior, "Cyber security strategy for Germany" (2011), 14.

Fidler, David, "Tinker, tailor, soldier, duqu: why cyber espionage is more dangerous than you think," *International Journal of Critical Infrastructures*, 5 (2012), 28–29.

Fidler, David, "Why the WTO is not an appropriate venue for addressing economic cyber espionage," Arms Control Law Blog (11 February 2013).

Fidler, David, "Economic cyber espionage and international law: controversies involving government acquisition of trade secrets through cyber technologies," *ASIL*, 17(10) (2013).

Fleck, Dieter, "Individual and state responsibility for intelligence gathering," *MJIL*, 28(3) (2007), 687–709.

Gellman, Barton and Laura Poitras, "U.S., British intelligence mining data from nine U.S. internet companies in broad secret program," *Washington Post* (2013).

Geneva Convention Relative to the Protection of Civilian Persons in Time of War (adopted on 12 August 1949, entered into force 21 October 1950) 75 U.N.T.S 287.

Gercke, Marco, *Understanding Cybercrime: Phenomena, Challenges and Legal Response*, Geneva: *ITU* (2012).

Gibson, William, *Neuromancer*, New York: Ace Pulishing (1984).

Glanz, James and Andrew W. Lehren, "NSA spied on allies, aid groups and businesses," *The New York Times* (2013).

Goldsmith, Jack L., "Against cyberanarchy," *University of Chicago Law Review*, 65(4) (1998), 1200.

Goldsmith, Jack L. and Eric Posner, *Limit of International Law*, Oxford: Oxford University Press (2005).

Gould, Wesley L. and Michael Barkun, *International Law and the Social Sciences*, Princeton: Princeton University Press (1970).

Greenwald, Glenn, Ewen MacAskill and Laura Poitras, "Edward Snowden: the whistleblower behind the NSA surveillance revelations," *Guardian* (2013).

Grotius, Hugo, *The Rights of War and Peace*, Book 3, edited by Knud Haakonssen, Indianapolis: Liberty Fund (2005).

Grotius, Hugo, *On the Law of War and Peace*, translated and edited by A. C. Campbell, Kitchener: Batoche Books (2001).

Gürbüz Usluel, Aslı E., *Anonim şirketlerde Ticari Sırrın Korunması*, İstanbul: Vedat (2009).

Guymon, CarrieLyn D. (ed.), *Digest of United States Practice in International Law*, US Department of State, Chapter 18 (2014), 738.

Halberstam, Manny, "Hacking back: reevaluating the legality of retaliatory cyberattacks," *The George Washington International Law Review*, 46 (2013), 199–237.

Hargrove, Susan and Kayla Marshall, *The Prospect of a Federal Trade Secret Claim*, North Carolina: Smith Anderson Law Firm (2015).

Hays Parks, W., "The international law of intelligence collection," in *National Security Law*, John Norton Moore and Robert F. Turner (eds.) Durham: Carolina Academic Press (1999).

Herbig, Katherine L. and Martin F. Wiskoff, *Espionage Against the United States by American Citizens 1947–2001*, Monterey, CA: Defense Personnel Security Research Center (2002).

Hickins, Michael, "Spying fears abroad hurt U.S. tech firms," *Wall Street Journal* (2014).

Hopkins, Shannon, "Cybercrime convention: a positive beginning to a long road ahead," *Journal of High Technology Law*, 2 (2003), 101–22.

Hung, Mark (ed.), "Leading the IoT," Gartner (2017).

Hurst, Daniel, "Australia has violated Timor-Leste's sovereignty, UN court told," *Guardian* (2014).

Hurst, James Williard, *The Growth of American Law: The Law Makers*, Boston: Little Brown and Company (1950).

Iasiello, Emilio, "Are cyber weapons effective military tools?," *Military and Strategic Affairs*, 7(1) (2015), 23–40.

Jarrett, H. Marshall and Michael W. Bailie, Prosecuting Computer Crimes, Office of Legal Education Executive Office for United States Attorneys (2015).

Johnson, David and David Post, "Law and borders – the rise of law in cyberspace," *Stanford Law Review*, 48 (1996).

Joint Communiqué – 2nd Canada-China High-Level National Security and Rule of Law Dialogue (2017).

Jones, Sam, "US spies engaged in industrial espionage will be jailed, says lawmaker," *Financial Times* (2014).

Keyser, Mike, "The Council of Europe Convention on cybercrime," *Journal of Transnational Law and Policy*, 12 (2003), 425–46.

Kindred, H. M., *International Law, Chiefly as Interpreted and Applied in Canada* 5th ed., Toronto: Emond Publishing (1993).

Kish, John and David Turns (eds.), *International Law and Espionage*, The Hague: Kluwer Law International (1995).

Kissel, Richard (ed.), *NIST Glossary of Key Information Security Terms*, Gaithersburg: National Institute of Standards and Technology (2013).

Kissinger, Henry, *World Order*, London: Penguin Books (2014).

Klabbers, Jan, *International Law*, Cambridge: Cambridge University Press (2013).

Knightley, Phillip, *The Second Oldest Profession: Spies and Spying in the Twentieth Century*, New York: W. W. Norton & Co. (1986).

Koh, Harold H., "International law in cyberspace," The USCYBERCOM Inter-Agency Legal Conference (2012).

Kuehl, Daniel T., "From cyber space to cyberpower: defining the problem," in Franklin D. Kramer, Stuart H. Starr and Larry K. Wentz, *Cyberpower and National Security*, Washington, DC: National Defense University Press (2009).

Kurtz, Georger, "Global energy cyberattacks: 'Night Dragon'", McAfee (2011).

Lang, Joe, "The protection of commercial trade secrets," *European Intellectual Property Review*, Vol 25/10 (2003).

Leahy, Joe, "Brazil's Petrobras to invest heavily in data security," *Financial Times* (2013).

Lichtfuss, Matt, "Cyber-espionage making headlines over past couple weeks," SurfWatchLabs (2016).

Lindsay, Jon R., Tai Ming Cheung and Derek S. Reveron (eds.), *China and Cybersecurity: Espionage, Strategy, and Politics in the Digital Domain*, Oxford: Oxford University Press (2015).

Lotrionte, Catherine, "Countering state-sponsored cyber economic espionage under international law," *North Carolina Journal of International Law*, 40 (2014), 443–541.

Mamiit, Aaron, "German government drops verizon contract in fear of U.S. espionage," *Tech Times* (2014).

Mandiant, "APT1 exposing one of China's cyber espionage units" (18 February 2013).

McAfee, "Global energy cyberattacks: 'Night Dragon'" (10 February 2011).

McAfee, "Net losses: estimating the global cost of cybercrime" (June 2014).

McAfee, Combating advanced persistent threats: how to prevent, detect, and remediate APTs, White Papers (2011).

Mclaughlin, Jenna, "Artificial intelligence will put spies out of work, too," *Foreign Policy* (2017).

Mclaughlin, Jenna, "The robots will run the CIA, too," *Foreign Policy* (2017).

Melnitzky, Alexander, "Defending America against Chinese cyber espionage through the use of active defenses," *Cardozo Journal of International Comparative Law* 20 (2012) 566.

Melzer, Nils, *Cyberwarfare and International Law*, Geneva: UNIDIR (2011).

Messmer, Ellen, "Cyber-espionage attacks threaten corporate data in new unrelenting ways," Network World (2011).

Miller, Claire Cain, "Revelations of NSA spying cost US tech companies," *New York Times* (2014).

Mitchell, Kate and Dapo Akande, "Espionage & good faith in treaty negotiations: *East Timor* v. *Australia*," *EJIL* Blog (2014).

Montevideo Convention (signed on 26 December 1933, entered into force on 26 December 1934).

Morin-Desailly, Catherine, Rapport D'information fait au nom de la mission commune d'information nouveau rôle et nouvelle stratégie pour l'Union européenne dans la gouverance mondiale de l'Internet, *Rapports Parlementaires* (2014).

Mundie, Craig, Speaking on the Future of Technology Conference Columbia University School of International and Public Affairs (2013) www.youtube. com/watch?v=tnojfzVv7eA (accessed 22 June 2015).

Murphy, Katharine and Lenore Taylor, "Timor-Leste spy case: witness held, and lawyer's office raided by ASIO," *Guardian* (2013).

Murray, Andrew, *Information Technology Law*, Oxford: Oxford University Press (2013).

Naim, Moises, *End of Power: From Boardrooms to Battlefields and Churches to States, Why Being in Charge Isn't What It Used To Be*, New York: Basic Books (2013).

NSA, In the Matter of Foreign Governments, Foreign Factions, Foreign Entities and Foreign-Based Political Organizations (2010).

Ohlin, Jens David, Kevin Govern and Claire Finkelstein, *Cyber War: Law and Ethics for Virtual Conflicts*, Oxford: Oxford University Press (2015).

Öktem, Akif Emre, *Uluslararası Teamül Hukuku*, İstanbul: Beta (2013).

Oppenheim, Lassa, *International Law, a Treatise II*, New York: Longmans (1912).

Oraison, André, "Le dol dans la conclusion des traités," *Revue Générale de Droit International*, 75(1971) 617–73.

Ottis, R. and P. Lorents, "Cyberspace: definition and implications," in *Proceedings of the 5th International Conference on Information Warfare and Security*, Dayton: Academic Publishing Limited (2010).

Owens, William A., Kenneth W. Dam and Herbert S. Lin (eds.), *Technology, Policy, Law, and Ethics Regarding U.S. Acquisition and Use of Cyberattack Capabilities*, Washington, DC: National Academic Press (2009).

Öztek, Selçuk, "Protection of trade secrets through ipr and unfair competition law," *AIPPIA* Yearbook Vol. 3 (2010), 467–77.

Paganini, Pierluigi, "Snowden reveals that China stole plans for a new F-35 air-craft fighter," *Security Affairs* (19 January 2015).

Paganini, Pierluigi, "FireEye World War C report – nation-state driven cyber attacks," Security Affairs RSS (3 October 2013) http://securityaffairs.co/wordpress/18294/security/fireeye-nation-state-driven-cyber-attacks.html (4 June 2018).

Parker, Warrington, "President Obama signs into law the Theft of Trade Secrets Clarification Act," Orrick News Alert (2013).

Paul, T. V., *Asymmetric Conflicts: War Initiation by Weaker Powers*, Cambridge: Cambridge University Press (1994).

PCIJ, Phosphates in Morocco, Judgment, Series A/B No. 74 (1938).

PCIJ, The Case of the S.S. Lotus, Judgment, Series A. No. 10 (1927).

Pehlivan, Oğuz Kaan, "İpin ucunu kaçırmak: NSA," *Analist Journal*, 34 (2013).

Pehlivan, Oğuz Kaan, "Siber dünya: gerçekler ve reel tehditler," *Analist Journal*, 31 (2013).

Pehlivan, Oğuz Kaan, "Siber saldırılar karşısında meşru müdafaa hakkı," *Kamu Hukuku Arşivi*, 17(1–2), *Adalet Yayınevi* (2017).

Pelican, Luke, "Peacetime cyberespionage: a dangerous, but necessary game," *CommLaw Conspectus*, 20 (2012), 363–90.

Philipp, Joshua, "The staggering cost of economic espionage against the US," *Epoch Times* (2013).

Poitras, Laura, Marcel Rosenbach and Holger Stark, "Codename 'Apalachee': how America spies on Europe and the UN," *Der Spiegel* (2013).

Protocol Additional to the Geneva Conventions of 12 August 1949, and relating to the Protection of Victims of International Armed Conflict (Protocol I) (Adopted 8 June 1977) 1125 U.N.T.S. 3.

Rayment, Sean, "Britain under attack from 20 foreign spy agencies including France and Germany," *The Telegraph* (2009).

Reed, Chris, *Internet Law: Text and Materials*, Cambridge: Cambridge University Press (2004).

Reinhold, Steven, "Good faith in international law," *UCL Journal of Law and Jurisprudence*, 2 (2013), 40–63, Bonn Research Paper on Public International Law No. 2/2013 (2013).

Reuter, Paul, *Introduction to the Law of Treaties*, New York: Routledge (1989).

Rid, Thomas, *Cyber War Will Not Take Place*, Oxford: Oxford University Press (2013), 37.

Rid, Thomas and Peter McBurney, "Cyber-weapons," *RUSI Journal*, 157(1) (2012), 6–13.

Ringsmose, Jens and Karsten Friis, *Conflict in Cyber Space*, New York: Routledge (2016).

Rogers, Michael, "Panel discussion 'rebooting trust? freedom v. security in cyberspace'," Munich Security Conference (31 February 2014).

Roscini, Marco, "World wide warfare – jus ad bellum and the use of cyber force," *Max Planck Yearbook of United Nations Law*, 14 (2010).

Roscini, Marco, *Cyber Operations and the Use of Force in International Law*, Oxford: Oxford University Press (2014).

Roscini, Marco, "Evidentiary issues in international disputes related to state responsibility for cyber operations," *Texas International Law Journal*, 50(2) (2015), 233–73.

Roudik, Peter, *Foreign Intelligence Gathering Laws*, Washington, DC: Law Library of Congress (2014).

Rousseff, Dilma, President of The Federative Republic Of Brazil, at the opening of the general debate of the 68th session of the United Nations General Assembly, New York (24 September 2013).

Rowe, Elizabeth A. and Sharon K. Sandeen, *Trade Secrecy and International Transactions Law and Practice*, Cheltenham: Edward Elgar (2015).

Saias, Marco Alexandre, "Unlawful acquisition of trade secrets by cyber theft: between the proposed directive on trade secrets and the directive on cyber attacks," *JIPLP*, 9(9) (2015), 721–29.

Sandvik, Kristin Bergtora, *Towards a Militarization of Cyberspace? Cyberwar as an Issue of International Law*, Oslo: PRIO Papers (2012).

Sattarova Feruza, Y. and Prof.Tao-hoon Kim, "IT security review: privacy, protection, access control, assurance and system security," *International Journal of Multimedia and Ubiquitous Engineering*, 2(2) (2007), 17–32.

Schachter, Oscar, *International Law in Theory and Practice*, Leiden: Martinus Nijhoff Publishers (1991).

Schmidt, Eric and Jared Cohen, *The New Digital Age: Reshaping the Future of People, Nations and Business*, New York: Vintge Books (2013).

Schmitt, Michael N., "Computer network attack and the use of force in international law: thoughts on a normative framework," *Columbia Journal of Transnational Law*, 37 (1999), 885–937.

Schmitt, Michael N. (ed.), *Tallinn Manual on the International Law Applicable to Cyber Warfare*, Cambridge: Cambridge University Press (2013).

Schmitt, Michael N., "Cyber responses 'by the numbers' in international law," *EJIL* (2015).

Schmitt, Michael N. (ed.), *Tallinn Manual 2.0 on the International Law Applicable to Cyber Operations*, Cambridge: Cambridge University Press (2017).

Schneier, Bruce, *Data and Goliath: The Hidden Battles to Collect Your Data and Control Your World*, New York: W. W. Norton & Company (2016).

Secureworks Counter Threat Unit Research Team, "BRONZE BUTLER targets Japanese enterprises" (12 October 2017) www.secureworks.com/research/bronze-butler-targets-japanese-businesses (accessed 20 December 2017).

Shackelford, Scott J., *Managing Cyber Attacks in International Law, Business, and Relations In Search of Cyber Peace*, Cambridge: Cambridge University Press (2014).

Shaw, Malcolm N., *International Law*, Cambridge: Cambridge University Press 6th edition (2008).

Simonite, Tom, "For superpowers, artificial intelligence fuels new global arms race," Wired (2017).

Singer, P. W. and Allan Friedman, *Cybersecurity and Cyberwar: What Everyone Needs To Know*, Oxford: Oxford University Press (2014).

Skinner, Christina Parajon, "An international law response to economic cyber espionage," *Connecticut Law Review*, 46 (2014).

Soto, Alonso and Brian Winter, "Saab wins Brazil jet deal after NSA spying sours Boeing bid," *Reuters* (2013).

Sperling, James (ed.) *Handbook of Governance and Security*, Cheltenham: Edward Elgar (2014).

Stahl, William M., "The uncharted waters of cyberspace: applying the principles of international maritime law to the problem of cybersecurity," *GJICLR*, 40 (2011).

Strate, Lance, "The varieties of cyberspace: problems in definition and delimitation," *Western Journal of Communication*, 63 (1999), 382–412.

Sulu, Muhammed, *Ticari Sırların Korunması*, İstanbul: On İki Levha Yayıncılık (2016).

Sutcliffe, David, "What are the current grand challenges of internet research," Oxford Internet Institute Blog (2016).

Tapper, Colin, *Computers and the Law*, London: Weidenfeld and Nicolson (1973).

Taylor, Paul, "Industrial espionage cyber style," *Financial Times* (8 November 2011).

Threat Connect and Defense Group Inc., "Project Camerashy: closing the aperture on China's unit 78020," ThreatConnect (2015).

Tsagourias, Nicholas and Russell Buchan (eds.), *Research Handbook on International Law and Cyberspace*, Cheltenham: Edward Elgar (2015).

Toren, Peter J., *Intellectual Property and Computer Crimes*, New York: Law Journal Press (2016).

Turkey's National Cyber Security and 2013–2014 Action Plan (2012).

UK Houses of Parliament, Cyber Security in the UK (2011).

UK Law Commission, "Legislating the criminal code: misuse of trade secrets," Law Commission Consultation Paper 15 (1997).

UNGA, Report of the Special Rapporteur on the promotion and protection of human rights and fundamental freedoms while countering terrorism A/HRC/14/46.

U.S. Department of Justice, "U.S. Charges Five Chinese Military Hackers with Cyber Espionage against U.S. Corporations and a Labor Organization for Commercial Advantage" (2014).

U.S. Department of Defence, Dictionary of Military and Associated Terms (12 April 2001) (as amended through August 26, 2008).

U.S. Department of Defence, Joint Publication 3–12, Cyberspace Operations (2013).

U.S. Department of Justice, U.S. Charges Five Chinese Military Hackers with Cyber Espionage against U.S. Corporations and a Labor Organization for Commercial Advantage (2014).

U.S. Department of Justice, U.S. Charges Five Chinese Military Hackers for Cyber Espionage against U.S. Corporations and a Labor Organization for Commercial Advantage (2014).

US Department of State, Digest of United States Practice in International Law, Chapter 18 (2014).

U.S.-China Economic and Security Review Commission, Hearing on Commercial Cyber Espionage and Barriers to Digital Trade in China, testimony of Jen Weedon (2015).

U.S. Chamber of Commerce, The Case for Enhanced Protection of Trade Secrets in the Trans-Pacific Partnership Agreement (2013).

Valentino-Devries, Jennifer and Danny Yadron, "Cataloging the world's cyberforces," *Wall Street Journal* (2015).

Vatis, Michael, "The Council of Europe Convention on Cybercrime," in *Proceedings of a Workshop on Deterring CyberAttacks: Informing Strategies and Developing Options for US Policy* Washington, DC: National Academic Press.

Villiger, Mark E., *Commentary on the 1969 Vienna Convention on the Law of Treaties*, Leiden: Martinus Nijhoff (2009).

Waldock, Humprey, "Fifth Report on the Law of the Treaties," *Yearbook of the International Law Commission* (1965).

Weber, Amalie, "The Council of Europe Convention on cybercrime," *Berkeley Technology Law Journal*, 18 (2014) 425–46.

Webster, Graham, Rogier Creemers, Paul Triolo and Elsa Kania, "China's plan to 'lead' in AI: purpose, prospects, and problems," New America (2017).

The White House, Fact Sheet, "President Xi Jinping's State Visit to the United States," Washington, DC: Office of the Press Secretary (2015).

Wiener, Norbert, *Cybernetics or the Control and Communication in the Animal and the Machine*, Massachusetts: MIT Press (1948).

Wilson, Bruce, "The WTO dispute settlement system and its operation: a brief overview of the first ten years," in Rufus Yerxa and Bruce Wilson (eds.), *Key Issues in WTO Dispute Settlement*, Cambridge: Cambridge University Press (2005) 16.

Wright, Quincy, "Espionage and the doctrine of non-intervention in internal affairs," *Essays on Espionage and International Law*, Ohio: Ohio State University Press (2008).

WTO, *A Handbook on the WTO Dispute Settlement System*, Cambridge: Cambridge University Press (2004).

Yearbook of International Law Commission, Vol. II (1) Third Report on State Responsibility, A/CN.4/440 (1991).

Yeh, Brian T., *Protection of Trade Secrets: Overview of Current Law and Legislation*, Washington, DC: Congressional Research Service (2016).

Yerxa, Rufus, "The power of the WTO dispute settlement system," in Rufus Yerxa and Bruce Wilson (eds.), *Key Issues in WTO Dispute Settlement*, Cambridge: Cambridge University Press (2005), 4.

Yoo, Christopher S., "Cyber espionage or cyber war? International law, domestic law, and self-protective measures," *Faculty Scholarship Paper*, 1540 (2015).

Yoo, John, "Counterintuitive: intelligence operations and international law," *MJIL*, 28 (2006), 625–38.

Young, Mark D., "National cyber doctrine: the missing link in the application of American cyber power," *Journal of National Security Law & Policy*, 173 (2010), 173–96.

Zemanek, Karl, "Economic warfare," in Rudolf Bernhardt, *Encyclopedia of Public International Law*, Vol. 3 Amsterdam: North Holland Publishing (1981), 158.

Ziolkowski, Katharina, "Peacetime cyber espionage – new tendencies in public international law," in Katharina Ziolkowski (ed.), *Peacetime Regime for State Activities in Cyberspace: International Law, International Relations and Diplomacy*, Tallinn: CCDCOE (2013).

Treaties and other legal documents

Agreement on Mutual Legal Assistance in Criminal Matters, U.S. – China (2000).

Agreement on Trade-Related Aspects of Intellectual Property Rights (TRIPS) (adopted 15 April 1994).

Australian Minister for Foreign Affairs & Special Minister of State, "Arbitration under the Timor Sea Treaty" (3 May 2013).

Draft articles on Responsibility of States for Internationally Wrongful Acts, with commentaries, *Yearbook of the International Law Commission*, 2(2) (2001).

Draft Convention on the Law of Treaties, Harvard Law School (1935).

Canadian Security Intelligence Service Act (Re) (F.C.), 2008 FC 301.

CCDCOE, Tallinn Manual on The International Law Applicable to Cyber Warfare (2013).

Council of Europe, Convention on Cybercrime, European Treaty Series – No. 185 (signed 23 November 2001, in effect 1 July 2004).

Economic Espionage Act, 18 USC § 1831 (1996).

European Council Framework Decision 2005/222/JHA of 24 February 2005 on attacks against information systems.

European Parliament and The Council, Directive 2013/40, "On Attacks Against Information Systems and Replacing Council Framework Decision 2005/222/JHA," *Official Journal of European Union* L218/8 (2013).

Foreign Intelligence Surveillance Act 50 U.S.C. sec. 1881a.

Geneva Convention Relative to the Protection of Civilian Persons in Time of War (adopted on 12 August 1949, entered into force 21 October 1950) 75 U.N.T.S.

Hague Convention on respecting the Laws and Customs of War on Law (adopted on 18 October 1907, entered into force 26 January 1910).

HPCR, *Manual on International Law Applicable to Air and Missile Warfare*, Harvard University (2009).

International Law Commission, Draft Articles on the Law of Treaties with commentaries (1966).

ICRC, The Montreux Document on Private Military and Security Companies (2009).

Marrakesh Agreement, Establishing the World Trade Organization, 15 April 1994.

Montevideo Convention (signed 26 December 1933, entered into force on 26 December 1934).

Protocol Additional to the Geneva Conventions of 12 August 1949, and relating to the Protection of Victims of International Armed Conflict (Protocol I) (Adopted 8 June 1977), 1125 U.N.T.S.

Timor Sea Treaty between the Government of East Timor and the Government of Australia, ATS 13 (adopted 20 May 2002. entered into force 2 April 2003).

Treaty on Open Skies (entered into force on 1 January 2002).

Treaty between Australia and The Democratic Republic of Timor-Leste on Certain Maritime Arrangements in The Timor Sea (adopted 12 January 2006, entry into force, 23 February 2007), ATS 12.

Turkish Criminal Code, Law with Nr. 5237 (passed on 26 September 2004, Official Gazette No. 25611 dated 12 October 2004).

Turkish Commercial Code, Law with Nr.6102 (accepted on 13 January 2011, Official Gazette No. 27846 dated on 14 February 2011).

Turkish Law on Personal Data Protection, Law with Nr.6698 (accepted on 24 March 2016 Official Gazette No. 29677 dated on 7 April 2016).

Turkish Draft Law on Trade Secrets, Banking Secrets and Client Secrets.

United Nations Charter, San Francisco (signed 26 June 1945, came into force 24 October 1945).

Uniform Law Commission, Uniform Trade Secret Act (1979, amended in 1985).

UKUSA Agreement (adopted on 10 May 1955).

UKUSA COMINT Agreement and Appendices Thereto (adopted 26 June 1951).

Vienna Convention on Diplomatic Relations (adopted 18 April 1961, entered into force 24 April 1964), 500 UNTS 95.

Vienna Convention on the Law of Treaties (adopted on 22 May 1969, entered into force on 27 January 1980), 1155 UNTS 331.

Wassenaar Arrangement on Export Controls for Conventional Arms and Dual-Use Goods and Technologies (accepted on 11–12 July 1996).

Index

Taylor & Francis eBooks

www.taylorfrancis.com

A single destination for eBooks from Taylor & Francis
with increased functionality and an improved user
experience to meet the needs of our customers.

90,000+ eBooks of award-winning academic content in
Humanities, Social Science, Science, Technology, Engineering,
and Medical written by a global network of editors and authors.

TAYLOR & FRANCIS EBOOKS OFFERS:

A streamlined
experience for
our library
customers

A single point
of discovery
for all of our
eBook content

Improved
search and
discovery of
content at both
book and
chapter level

REQUEST A FREE TRIAL
support@taylorfrancis.com

Routledge
Taylor & Francis Group

CRC Press
Taylor & Francis Group

For Product Safety Concerns and Information please contact our EU
representative GPSR@taylorandfrancis.com
Taylor & Francis Verlag GmbH, Kaufingerstraße 24, 80331 München, Germany

www.ingramcontent.com/pod-product-compliance
Ingram Content Group UK Ltd.
Pitfield, Milton Keynes, MK11 3LW, UK
UKHW021423080625
459435UK00011B/137